THE SUCCESSFUL MANAGER'S GUIDE TO BUSINESS PLANNING

7 Practical Steps to Producing Your Best Ever Business Plan

THE SUCCESSFUL MANAGER'S GUIDE TO BUSINESS PLANNING

7 Practical Steps to Producing Your Best Ever Business Plan

David Freemantle

McGRAW-HILL BOOK COMPANY
London · New York · St Louis · San Francisco · Auckland · Bogotá
Caracas · Lisbon · Madrid · Mexico · Milan · Montreal
New Delhi · Panama · Paris · San Juan · Sao Paulo
Singapore · Sydney · Tokyo · Toronto

658 4035 FRE

022 03

Published by   658 · 4012 FRE
McGRAW-HILL Book Company Europe
Shoppenhangers Road, Maidenhead, Berkshire SL6 2QL, England
Telephone: 0628 23432
Fax 0628 770224

British Library Cataloguing in Publication Data

Freemantle, David
  Successful Manager's Guide to Business
  Planning: 7 Practical Steps to Producing Your Best Ever Business Plan
  I. Title
  658.4012

ISBN 0-07-707845-4

Library of Congress Cataloging-in-Publication Data
This data is available from the Library of Congress, Washington DC, USA.

1234 BL 9765

Typeset by TecSet Ltd, Wallington, Surrey
and printed and bound in Great Britain by Biddles Ltd., Guildford and King's Lynn.

CONTENTS

V

ACKNOWLEDGEMENTS

The efforts of an author are never sufficient to bring a book to publication. Behind the scenes are a number of people who invariably make an important contribution to the finished version. I would therefore like to thank all those who have given me time and furnished me with documentation to help complete this book.

First, I would like to thank Kate Allen from McGraw-Hill for her help and encouragement. Without her this book would not have got off the ground. I am also indebted to the other countless people at McGraw-Hill who have played their part in publishing this book.

Second, I would like to thank a number of people who have provided me with documentation which they have allowed me to freely use in this book. These are Brian Binley of BCC Marketing Services Ltd, David Scott of Windsor Leisure Pool, Richard Wilkinson of Bedfordshire County Council and Karen Ann Sisko of *Success Magazine* in New York. Furthermore, I would like to thank Graham Hall of Lloyds Bank who devoted time to talking me through the Lloyds approach and introducing me to Brian Binley.

Third, I would like to thank Jean Yabsley in our Superboss office at Windsor for keeping things moving with her effective efforts on the administrative side.

Finally, I would like to mention my wife, Mechi, for all her support and as usual exercising her supreme skills as a proofreader to improve the quality of my writing.

INTRODUCTION

I

❝People can be themselves only in small, comprehensible groups.❞

E.F. Schumacher, *Small is Beautiful* 1973

❝As our top-heavy, centralized institutions die, we are rebuilding from the bottom up. Decentralization creates more centers. That means more opportunities and more choices for individuals.❞

John Naisbitt, *Megatrends* 1982

❝The massive, vertically integrated enterprise, the giant factory fit for the ages—is dead. Beware of big, even network big, in a world come unhinged.❞

Tom Peters, *Liberation Management* 1992

The end of centralized bureaucratic organizations is near. Or so some pundits would have it. What is clear is that during the 1990s more and more organizations are decentralizing into fully empowered business units. The process of business planning is therefore becoming an increasingly important tool in the armoury of modern day managers.

One lesson from the 1980s was that large centralized organizations tend to have a constraining effect on their employees, stifling creativity and innovation and, in the long term, rendering them less able to compete with more progressive but smaller-scale businesses. Hence we saw the rise, apparently out of nowhere, of companies such as Virgin, Body Shop and Apple.

There is much evidence to suggest that the larger an organization becomes the larger the probability that it loses touch with its customers and their requirements, thus creating opportunities for adventurous

*'Few men have any next; they live from
hand to mouth, without plan, and are ever at
the end of their line, and after each action
wait for an impulse from abroad.'*
Ralph Waldo Emerson

The business plan represents a clear articulation of the modern manager's vision, the way forward to achieving it, and the risks involved.

Essentially it embodies a manager's view of his or her business—as it is now, as it has been in the past, and as it will be in the future.

FIGURE 1.1

entrepreneurs to capture substantial shares of markets which the larger organizations traditionally took for granted as theirs.

The solution is obvious and is now being pursued by many. It is a solution expounded by E. Fritz Schumacher in *Small is Beautiful* in the 1970s, by John Naisbitt in *Megatrends* in the 1980s and by Tom Peters in *Liberation Management* in the 1990s.

To reduce organizations to relatively small autonomous 'business units' capable of succeeding in a fast-moving and eccentric market-place requires highly effective managers with a range of skills not traditionally found in large organizations.

Business planning is one of those skills. It is a process of articulation. Modern managers need to be visionaries; they need to have the courage to pursue the massive challenges represented by their visions as well as be prepared to take the risks involved in this pursuit. Too many traditional managers baulk at such risk taking, limiting themselves to the comforts of a status quo which perpetuates practices which alienate not only their customers but their staff as well. Just look at the way many managers still pursue the traditional method of performance appraisal and merit pay—a practice which is, as a growing amount of research evidence proves, ineffective.

The business plan represents a clear articulation of the modern manager's vision, the way forward to achieving it, and the risks involved. Essentially it embodies a manager's view of his or her business, as it is now, as it has been in the past, and as it will be in the future.

If you are a manager working in a large organization which is trying to restructure into decentralized business units then this book is aimed at you. Such decentralization will present you with a set of business planning problems not encountered by others running self-contained small businesses—for example problems relating to overheads or central charges, internal competition, internal trading and inadequate management information. Frequent reference will be found to these issues in this book.

WHAT MANAGERS SAY:

◆ 'I found the business planning process incredibly useful in helping me understand what my business unit is all about.'

◆ 'Our service is being market tested. To be honest before this happened I just took it for granted that what we did was what people wanted. Preparing a business plan has meant we have had to justify our existence in real terms.'

◆ 'I found writing a business plan a terrible struggle, but it forced me to think about my area of responsibility in a way I hadn't before. I've learnt a lot and think we will be able to manage better as a result.'

◆ 'Preparing our business plan was a useful if time-consuming exercise, well worth it in the end. It opened our eyes about our business and helped us focus on developing a clear sense of direction.'

◆ 'It forced us to address key issues which we had been putting on the back-burner for too long.'

(Comments made by managers after attending programmes of training on how to produce business plans.)

FIGURE 1.2

Other books on business planning, and there are many of them, tend to be aimed at the manager of the small self-contained business seeking investment funds. If you are one of these you will also find value in this book even though its perspective is slanted towards managers of business units working in larger organizations. The process of establishing a vision and deriving from it a set of quantified strategic priority objectives will be useful to all managers.

You will also benefit if you are a manager in the public sector. Increasingly public sector organizations are being put onto a commercial footing by subjecting the services they provide to competitive tendering or market testing. Again this requires the development of business thinking throughout the organization. Business planning is a vital tool which will help in this developmental process.

To write a first-class business plan does not require the skills of a qualified accountant. In fact many managers are not proficient in financial analysis—quite rightly, they rely on the professionals to help them. This book, therefore, makes no attempt to induct you into the complexities of accountancy conventions or to instruct you on how to present accounts of profit and loss, cash flow or balance sheets. All that is required, in the first instance, is the production of some crude projections derived from your visionary strategic objectives. From then on you are advised to seek the help of your financial adviser to convert your raw projections into refined figures which will be acceptable to those from whom you are seeking approval for your plan.

The next chapter outlines the overall business planning process and as such can be used as a self-contained summary of the whole book. In subsequent chapters you will be guided through a preliminary step before being asked to take the seven key steps to producing your best ever business plan.

Comments about this book are very welcome and should be addressed to the author at Superboss Ltd, 5 High Street, Windsor, Berkshire, SL4 1LD, UK.

BUSINESS PLANNING THINKING PROCESS

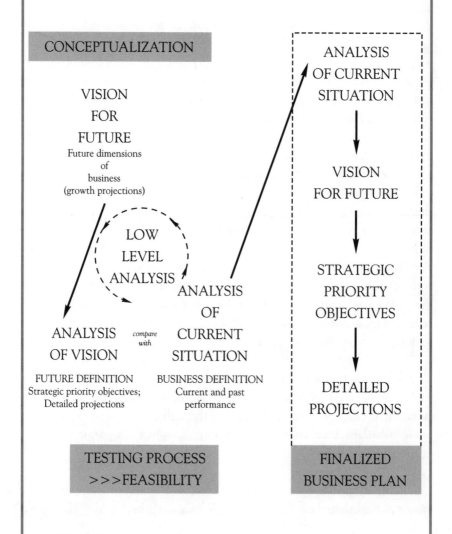

FIGURE 2.1

THE BUSINESS PLANNING PROCESS

❝Men don't plan to fail—they fail to plan.❞

William J. Siegel

This chapter introduces the overall Seven-step Business Planning Process which is explained in more detail in the following chapters. As such this chapter is a summary of the overall process. Furthermore, it introduces the seven keys required for successful business planning as well as a number of other important concepts to be used in the process.

The process of business planning can prove to be both therapeutic and cathartic. It is undeniably hard work but ultimately exceptionally rewarding. It will 'cleanse' your thinking about your business and thus help you develop your approach to it. In undertaking business planning you will learn a lot more about your business and thus acquire more confidence in how to manage it.

Without a business plan you can only 'react' to events. As such your achievements will be limited. A business plan helps you focus on the future and identify a clear course of action to lead you there.

The thinking process is quite straightforward. It starts with the conceptualization of a vision and then moves through an iterative cycle of review and analysis to the establishment of strategic priority objectives supported by detailed projections (see Fig. 2.1). The iterative cycle is simply a matter of analysing and clarifying your projections for the future and, to ensure feasibility, comparing these with an analysis of the current situation and recent performance.

DEFINING YOUR BUSINESS

Some basic questions:

◆ What are the business's:
   —outputs (i.e. products, services)?
   —inputs?
   —assets?
   —liabilities?

◆ What is the business's
   —market?
   —segment, share of market?

◆ Who are the business's:
   —customers?
   —competitors?
   —suppliers?

◆ What has the business recently achieved?

◆ What are the main capabilities (strengths) of the business?

◆ What are the business's inherent weaknesses?

◆ What is the financial situation (i.e. revenue, costs, cash flows, profits, balance sheet, etc.)?

What really makes your business unique?

FIGURE 2.2

PRELIMINARY STEP DETERMINING THE PURPOSE OF YOUR BUSINESS PLAN

Before you embark on the process of preparing a business plan you need to determine the purpose of the plan and who it is aimed at. Is it solely for the use of you and your team to help you manage more effectively, or is it aimed at a bank manager or venture capitalist to obtain funds for expansion, or is the target audience a senior executive in your organization whose approval you seek?

STEP I DEFINING YOUR BUSINESS

Having determined the purpose of the plan and the intended readership, **Step 1** is to define your current business as well as summarize your recent past performance. The latter is effectively your 'track record' and will help establish credibility with your readers and those whose approval you seek.

Defining your current business is a matter of answering some basic questions and where appropriate quantifying the responses (see Fig. 2.2).

OUTPUTS AND INPUTS

In defining your business you will need to be very clear about its 'outputs' and 'inputs'. In traditional centralized organizations managers tend not to have real accountability for managing a self-contained set of inputs to deliver the required outputs. The ultimate control of certain inputs (such as people, money, accommodation) is retained centrally. Such managers have little scope to vary inputs to deliver outputs without obtaining approvals from more senior management. As a result, lines of accountability tend to become blurred between the centre of the organization and line managers operating locally who frequently feel constrained. When you manage your own business you do not have these constraints. This is now recognized in many large progressive organizations (including those within the public sector) which have been restructured into business units to give managers real accountability for both inputs and outputs.

THE MEANING OF BUSINESS— THE VITAL LINKS

Business means

➥ **Competition** for

➥ **Customers** making a

➥ **Choice** of

➥ **Outputs** earning you

➥ **Revenue** from

➥ **Inputs**

thus leading to

➥ **Profits** and

➥ **Survival/growth**

All these links have to be defined for your business

FIGURE 2.3

While it is easy to define manufactured products in terms of units of output (for example, an automobile component) it is far more difficult to determine the unit of output for an internal service such as personnel, finance or building services. The concept of output, therefore, is one that many managers in large organizations struggle with in preparing their business plans. Consequently many business plans produced within organizations are no more than a string of ill-defined objectives with no reference to quantified outputs or inputs. Frequently the business planning process is totally divorced from that of budgeting and budgets which, when finally approved, take little account of the outputs to be delivered or of strategic changes planned.

QUANTIFICATION OF OUTPUTS

A key to the business planning process therefore is the quantification of outputs. It is an essential part of **Step 1** in defining your business. If you cannot conceptualize and quantify the outputs you are required to deliver, you cannot operate or think like a business manager.

The term 'business' is inextricably linked with that of 'competition'. In the commercial world a customer makes a competitive choice when purchasing an output supplied by a business. If you do not know and are unable to quantify the outputs supplied to your customers, you cannot effectively be in business, nor manage a business unit.

Defining and quantifying outputs enables you to price them, and relate the revenue earned to the cost of production and delivery. Without such a pricing mechanism costs will inevitably get out of control as there is no measure of what is being delivered in relation to the allocated budget. This is what has happened traditionally in many large public sector organizations and is why many are moving towards a business approach with internal trading, compulsory competitive tendering and market testing.

The more clearly you define your current business and past performance the more effective a launch pad you have for developing your vision of the future.

CAUTION! THE DANGER OF HALF-BAKED VISIONS

AVOID

◆ **Meaningless sets of words**—clichés, platitudes, bland statements and wish-lists such as:
  'The best customer service'
  'The highest quality'

◆ **Slogans which cannot be lived up to**—such as:
  'Caring for you today'

◆ **Hostages to fortune**—a vision totally alien to customers' or staff's current perceptions of the business, such as:
  'We pride ourselves on serving you'

◆ **Fantasies**—impossible dreams which can never be realized and will be viewed by all as being ridiculous, such as:
  'To become the biggest and the best'

◆ **Statements which staff cannot relate to:**

A vision must have meaning for every single member of staff so that each one can contribute towards its achievement

FIGURE 2.4

NOTIONAL FIGURES

Sometimes data will not be available when you are defining your current business. In these cases you should use 'notional' figures which are based on your best estimates of what the real figures would be if you knew them. 'Notionality' is key to the business planning process. All future projections, by definition, are based on notional figures (given that the future is always unknown and at best can only be estimated using clear assumptions). The use of notional figures in business planning allows you to present a total, rather than incomplete, picture of how you see the business now and in the future.

The set of assumptions you use to establish notional figures effectively represents your business 'risk'. (There are no inherent risks in known figures based on accurate measures.)

STEP 2   FUTURE THINKING

Developing your vision for the future is **Step 2**. It is perhaps the most exciting and energizing aspect of the business planning process and one that is often neglected by busy managers running around reacting to today's events.

Step 2 therefore is to clarify your personal thinking about the future of the business for which you are accountable. You will probably need to have several (iterative) passes at developing your vision and most importantly you will need to involve your team in this process.

There is no set way for establishing a vision. However, many managers prefer to take their team away to some pleasant hotel for a couple of days to draw up a picture of the future as they see it.

While the process can be exciting, there are inherent dangers. The main one is that the vision is a meaningless set of words of no practical consequence for the future (Fig. 2.4).

VALUES AND BELIEFS

THE KEY QUESTION:

◆ WHAT DOES YOUR BUSINESS REALLY STAND FOR?

FIGURE 2.5

Ideally the vision should be an exciting and challenging focus for the future direction of your business. It is essential that the vision can be converted into a range of key business activities which will lead to its achievement. These will be your strategic priority objectives.

VALUES AND BELIEFS

Coupled with the vision should be a clear statement laying out your 'values' and 'beliefs' about what your business really stands for. Values are expressions of what is really important to you personally in your business, while beliefs are the immutable set of principles upon which you base your everyday business practice. Values and beliefs are inextricably linked and should be totally compatible with the vision. For example, to declare that 'caring for staff' is a core value in your business and then, a little later, to announce, without consultation, that a pay-cut or redundancy is to take place would send conflicting signals through your organization and diminish your credibility.

STEP 3   DEVELOPING YOUR PLAN

Step 3 of the business planning process is to take your vision, together with the 'strategic priority objectives' you have established and quantify them.

In other words, **Step 3** is to crystallize your vision as a set of projected figures and measures which will reflect your intended achievements. You will need to analyse each strategic priority objective and assess the financial implications of implementing it. From this process you will be able to develop a set of financial projections which reflect the progressive results you plan to achieve in pursuit of your vision. It is important that these financial projections are integrated with any budget formulation process you currently have. As mentioned before, in too many organizations the process of preparing and deciding upon budgets is seen as a separate activity to that of business planning.

MAKE YOUR BUSINESS PLAN FIREPROOF!

TEST YOUR PLAN TO DESTRUCTION

◆ MAKE SURE THAT:
EVERY FIGURE
EVERY WORD
EVERY ASSUMPTION
IN YOUR PLAN CAN BE FULLY
EXPLAINED AND SUBSTANTIATED

◆ PULL YOUR BUSINESS PLAN APART AND
PUT IT BACK TOGETHER AGAIN

HAVE OTHER PEOPLE PICK IT TO PIECES

MAKE IT FIREPROOF!

FIGURE 2.6

FINANCIAL IMPACT

To make your business plan credible, it is essential that the impact it has on revenue, costs, balance sheets, cash flows and profits is clearly spelt out. You will therefore need to have an early consultation with your financial adviser during **Step 3**, especially if you are not a financial expert. Each assumption you make, and each notional figure derived from it, needs to be clearly stated.

Even if you are working in a public sector organization you can still produce these projections. You do not have to be profit-oriented to have a business plan. In these cases it is important to demonstrate that you can balance your books, i.e.

Total value of outputs = Total costs.

STEP 4   CHALLENGING YOUR PLAN

Step 4 is to take the first version of your plan and challenge every single statement and figure in it, effectively testing it to destruction. This can be the most painful part of the business planning process. The critical task is to ensure that every figure, every word, every assumption in your plan can be fully explained and substantiated. Expressed another way, your business plan must be 'fireproof'. To achieve this you must be prepared to pull apart the first version of your business plan and put it back together again—as well as have other people, such as your financial adviser and your team, pick it to pieces (Fig. 2.6).

At this stage your plan is only a rough draft containing raw data and you need not worry about presenting it in a polished form. The only requirement is to ensure that your figures are intelligible to the people challenging them.

Having fully tested your projections, you will now need to pull all your data and information together in the form of an intelligible, easy-to-read and well-presented final version which is absolutely credible and totally convincing as far as your intended readers are concerned.

As equally important as what you say is how you say it

As equally important as what you say is how you say it

<u>As equally important as what you say is how you say it</u>

As equally important as <u>what</u> you say is <u>how</u> you say it

FIGURE 2.7

STEP 5   WRITING YOUR PLAN

Step 5, therefore, is to write your plan. In Chapter 9 a template (Fig. 9.1) is provided to help you with this. This template suggests section headings for your plan and what should be included in it. However you might well want to use a different structure depending on the nature of the business you are in and what you want to say. In other words, the template is provided as an aid and should not be used slavishly.

STEP 6   PRESENTING YOUR PLAN

You will recall that the preliminary step was to identify who the plan was aimed at. **Step 6** is to concentrate your energies on the best way of presenting your written plan to your target audience. It will not be sufficient just to send the plan to the appropriate people and wait and see what happens. You will be seeking to use the plan to achieve a specific end result. What is that result? What is the best way of convincing 'the powers that be' to support your plan? Who should be present? Who should present? Do you need a half-day seminar based on a slide presentation summarizing your plan or simply a one-hour walk-through with the appropriate person?

How you present and sell the plan is critical. A lot of hard work can be wasted unless you can get this step right.

STEP 7   IMPLEMENTATION AND REVIEW

Finally, you will need to consider how to review progress in implementing your plan once you have achieved your immediate objective of getting it approved. A plan is meaningless unless it is used as a working document for control purposes. To be effective, therefore, you need to establish a proper monitoring process to measure progress. This should be referred to in the business plan.

Step 7 is the final one in the business planning process and is critical if your plan is to have any credibility. Thus from time to time you will need to set some time aside to re-evaluate your plan, and update it and amend it as appropriate. It is a cliché, but probably true, that a plan will be out of date as soon as it is made. Even so your business plan should provide a clear sense of direction for your business and, while you might well need to vary the 'route' from time to time, your overall vision and strategic priority objectives should not change. Such changes of route arise invariably from unforeseen circumstances and a reassessment of 'how' you are going to achieve your vision.

The business planning process therefore becomes an ongoing and essential part of your management approach.

THE SEVEN KEYS

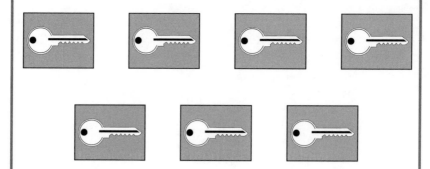

◆ THINKING BUSINESS

◆ UNIQUENESS

◆ VISION AND BELIEF

◆ OUTPUTS AND INPUTS

◆ CREDIBILITY AND RISK

◆ TARGETED STYLE

◆ INDESTRUCTIBILITY

FIGURE 3.1

THE SEVEN KEYS

> ❝*"Business" is a magical word, it turns out. It implies autonomy, practicality, action-taking, self-sufficiency and self-responsibility. In our biggest bureaucracies (private and public) these ideas have been absent for too long.*❞
>
> Tom Peters, *Liberation Management* 1992

There are seven keys to success when it comes to preparing and writing your business plan. These keys are shown on the page opposite (Fig. 3.1) and each one of them is then explained a little further in the rest of this chapter.

As you develop your business plan, step by step, try to recall each of these keys and see how they relate to what you are doing. Keep asking yourself questions such as:

◆ Am I really **thinking like a business person**, conscious of the bottom line all the time? And does this come through in the plan?

◆ Am I really clear about what is **unique** about the business and does the business plan portray that uniqueness adequately?

◆ Does my **vision** for the business really come alive in the plan? Is it sufficiently vivid?

◆ Have I focused enough on the core parameters of **outputs and inputs**?

◆ Is the plan **credible**? Have I taken sufficient account of the **risks** involved to be able to persuade others to support the plan?

INVERTING THE TRIANGLE

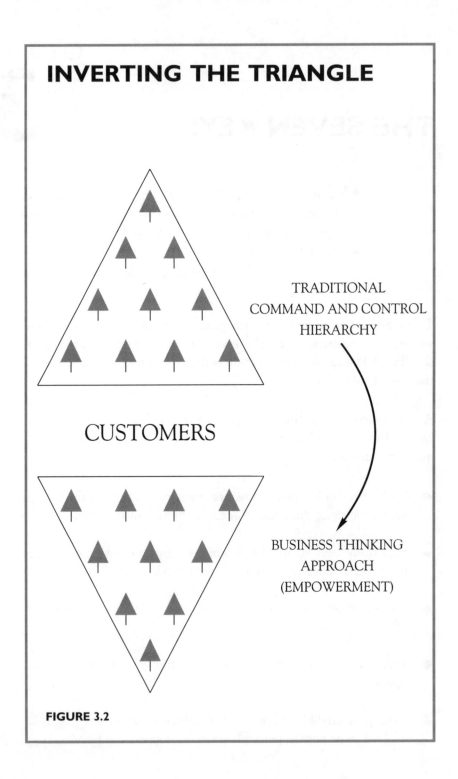

TRADITIONAL
COMMAND AND CONTROL
HIERARCHY

CUSTOMERS

BUSINESS THINKING
APPROACH
(EMPOWERMENT)

FIGURE 3.2

◆ Have I **targeted the style** of the plan on the required audience so that they will be turned on by it as opposed to being immediately switched off?

◆ Is the plan **indestructible**? In other words, can it withstand the most rigorous scrutiny so that every fact, figure and word can be maintained under sustained challenge?

THINKING BUSINESS

There is no point in having a 'business' plan unless you think of your area of responsibility as a business and feel empowered to run it like a business. Unless you do this, you may as well just have a plan. In other words, for business planning to be meaningful and effective the word 'business' has to have real meaning for you.

Very few managers who write business plans have total autonomy over their business. In fact only those who effectively own their business can have such autonomy.

In large organizations, where autonomies are much restricted, managers tend to think in terms of the traditional 'command and control' hierarchy rather than in terms of running their own business.

Yet to write a successful business plan it is essential for you to act as a fully empowered business person. This means that you have to imagine that you have total autonomy over your own area of responsibility. It means that you have to account not only for every pound of input cost but also for the revenue this generates.

IMAGINE TOTAL ACCOUNTABILITY

For example, if you owned your business you would be totally accountable for all office and accommodation costs and would therefore be able to make business decisions as to whether to lease space at £15 per square foot in location A as opposed to £12 per square foot in location B. Such a decision inevitably would have an impact on your profitability.

ACCOUNTABILITIES

List here the decisions for which you are currently accountable

List here the additional decisions you require to be fully accountable for the business you run

Use the business plan to highlight and justify the additional decisions you require to achieve your vision

FIGURE 3.3

In many large organizations so-called business managers have no idea of their office and accommodation costs—they are hidden in central charges or allocated overheads. As a consequence space can be squandered, as there is no real assessment by the local business manager of the impact of this cost on profitability. Alternatively there are conflicts with some managers at the centre over the best use of space. All this constrains managers from 'thinking business' and competing effectively on comparable terms. To encourage 'business thinking' many organizations are now moving towards internal trading, where business managers are charged directly for services such as offices and accommodation.

IMAGINE IT IS YOUR OWN MONEY

Another aspect of thinking business is to imagine that it is your own money you are spending. For example, it is all too easy in a large organization to plead a case for an additional member of staff. When you own your business you tend to say to yourself, 'If I spend £15 000 on this extra person my own income will be reduced by £15 000 unless this person generates additional revenue to cover this cost'. In other words, to think business you have to think in terms of 'added value'. You continually have to ask yourself, 'What revenue (value) does this person generate for the business?' It should be a standard management discipline to quantify every decision you make in these terms. It is simply a matter of relating all your decisions on inputs (and costs) to the outputs and revenues generated.

Say you are an accountant charging £80 per hour. It is relatively easy to calculate the revenue generated by hiring a secretary. For a start this secretary may well release you from 10 hours administration per week (thus enabling you to earn an additional £800 of fees per week). Also, you will enhance the quality of your response to customers by having someone to answer the telephone. This in itself will generate additional revenue.

RELATE EXPENDITURE TO REVENUE

Thinking business, therefore, means seeing all expenditure in terms of the revenue that it generates. It means assessing the direct and indirect

THE ESSENTIAL CONNECTION

EXPENDITURE → REVENUE

INPUT → OUTPUT

FREEDOM TO CONNECT!

FIGURE 3.4

impact of all costs on profitability—both in the short term as well as in the long term.

In this way you can establish much more effective control of the business you manage and, accordingly, produce better bottom line results for your organization.

Thinking business means creating as many freedoms as possible to make decisions to achieve success in your business. The more constraints placed on you internally by the organization, the less freedom you will have and the less able you will be to think in a businesslike way. The issue can be forced by the use of business planning and by inserting in the plan notional figures for costs over which currently you are allowed no control.

CAPITAL INVESTMENT

In thinking business the same principle applies to capital investment. It is not enough merely to make out a case to your bosses to have the office re-equipped and refurbished. The case has to be presented, through business planning, in terms of the added value re-equipment and refurbishment will bring to the quality of your business. Customers do make judgements based on what they experience. An untidy, dirty and cramped reception area with dilapidated copiers, telephones, filing cabinets and fax machines tells customers a lot about the business—it forces them to think about the quality of the service they are getting. It is not difficult to present a case for the additional revenue that a re-equipment and refurbishment will achieve. Once approved, it is only right that you, as a business manager, are held accountable for the additional outputs and revenue this investment will bring.

CUSTOMER SERVICE AND STAFF

Thinking business also requires an obsession with customer service. No business can survive unless the person running it is passionately committed to doing the very best for each and every customer. This obsession, this passion should show through in your business thinking and in your business plan.

CUSTOMER SERVICE AND STAFF: QUESTIONS

Customers

◆ What are their requirements of you now?

◆ What do they expect of you now?

◆ What will their requirements be in the future?

◆ What will they expect of you in the future?

Staff

◆ What are your requirements of them now?

◆ What do you expect of them now?

◆ What will your requirements be in the future?

◆ What will you expect of them in the future?

◆ What are their requirements of you now?

◆ What do they expect of you now?

◆ What will their requirements be in the future?

◆ What will they expect of you in the future?

Your plan should take account of the answers to these questions

FIGURE 3.5

Equally important is your attitude towards those you employ. You cannot care for your customers unless you care for your staff. This also is a key part of your business thinking which should be reflected in your business plan.

IN SUMMARY

Before you start work on your business plan you have to view your area of responsibility as if it were your own business and as if you were running it yourself. Furthermore you have to imagine that your livelihood depends directly on the revenues generated by the decisions you make.

To achieve this not only requires a mind clearly focused on revenue generation through shrewd management of costs, but also a deep-rooted obsession with motivating your people to provide the very best for your business's customers.

Unless you think this way you will not be able to produce a credible business plan nor manage in a businesslike way.

UNIQUENESS

To be successful, your business has to be unique. Your business plan has to demonstrate that uniqueness.

Uniqueness is the key to any business success and in preparing your business plan you will need to be 100 per cent clear about what makes your own business unique.

It is uniqueness which will commend your business to your customers, your staff, your bosses, your shareholders and the public at large.

This does not necessarily mean that the product you sell has to be unique. After all who can distinguish between different brands of petrol? What makes a business unique is a complex set of characteristics relating to product, service, market share, customer base, customer relationships, tangible assets, intellectual property, location, staff

THE SERVICE ENVELOPE

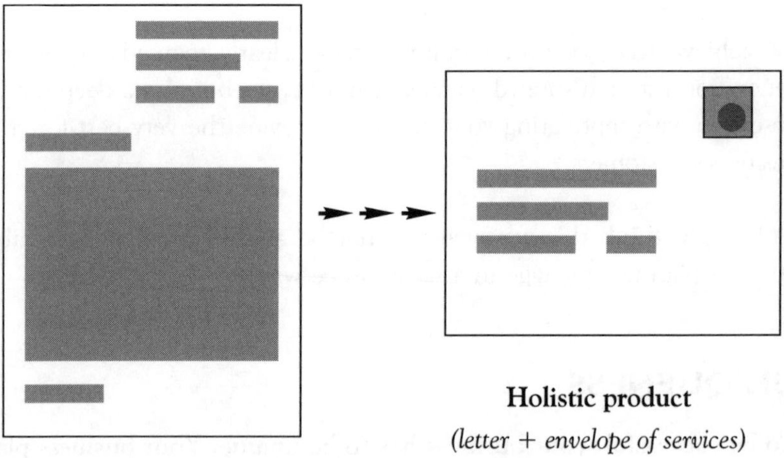

Core product
(letter)

Holistic product
(letter + envelope of services)

FIGURE 3.6

expertise, distribution network, information and data as well as, of course, financial circumstances.

Your business plan should be a compelling study of what is unique about your business today as well as historically and—most importantly—in the future.

No individual will ever support a business plan which reads like any other business plan and which describes a business which cannot be differentiated from another.

CORE PRODUCT—HOLISTIC PRODUCT

While the product you offer may well be identical to those of your competitors, what can be unique are other factors such as the exceptionally positive relationships you have with your customers, as well as the service and facilities you provide for them. Such characteristics of your business are of immense value and should be highlighted in your business plan. You could argue, of course, that while the core product is identical to that of your competitors the actual product is a 'holistic' combination of core product and exceptional service. Thus, though the core product may be petrol, the actual product is a holistic combination of petrol, price discounts or free gifts, location, ease of access, customer service, and additional features such as shopping facilities and toilets at the service station. As such, everyday core products can be developed into holistic products which are competitively unique. Some people describe this as developing the 'service envelope' containing the core product.

Focusing on uniqueness enables you to plan for its development. You may well recruit graduates with similar qualifications, but your plan will be to develop each one to possess an unrivalled and unique set of competencies of inestimable value to your business.

WHAT MAKES A BANK UNIQUE?

The concept of uniqueness seems so obvious that it is surprising that few businesses consider it. For example I suffer frequent frustrations with my bank. In a rare fit of pique I once approached a rival bank with a view to switching my account. The lady who saw me was their local 'small business account manager'. While I was dissatisfied with my bank, I did ask her what was unique about her bank (the qualities that would make me become a satisfied customer). She was unable to provide a credible answer, feebly responding that there was little to choose between the big four banks. Needless to say, I did not switch my account. Better the devil you know!

FIGURE 3.7

FOCUS ON COMPONENTS AND CHARACTERISTICS

The business planning process enables you to concentrate on each vital component of your business, and assess how unique its characteristics are and how to develop them further. Unless you do so your business will lapse into mediocrity and, consequently, prove no match for your competitors. In defining uniqueness you are defining the distinguishing capabilities of your business.

In the selling situation it is critical to establish pretty quickly in the mind of your potential customer what is unique about your business and what you are offering. In my workshops I often test managers by asking them to make a five-minute sales pitch to me (as if I were a potential customer). Unless you can articulate what is special about your business in summary form you cannot sell effectively. Few customers at the initial sales stage are prepared to devote time to long-winded managers who cannot express with passion what is unique about their business and the products and services on offer.

FOCUS ON UNIQUE SELLING POINT

The same applies to potential investors or acquirers as to customers. Imagine you own the business you manage and that you aim to retire in three years' time and sell the business. What would the potential purchaser be buying? Nobody buys a business unless you can demonstrate it is unique.

Business planning is an essential tool for demonstrating the uniqueness of your business and how you plan to develop it.

As you work through the seven steps of the business planning process continually ask yourself, 'Will this develop the uniqueness of my business?' The more often you answer 'Yes', the more likely your business plan will prove credible and your business ultimately successful.

VISION

A vision must:

◆ Genuinely reflect your deep-rooted ambitions for the business

◆ Be challenging and inspiring

◆ Be a clear and vivid statement of where you want to take the business

FIGURE 3.8

VISION AND BELIEF

Your vision for the business and belief about it should be at the heart of your business plan. Everything else flows from this—your conviction about the future of your business.

A business plan without an expression of vision and belief can be no more than an academic treatise resulting from an intellectual exercise. Business planning is more than an intellectual exercise, it is an expression of your personal beliefs about the future of the business and how you see it (your vision).

Many will tell you that business is more an art form than a science. Business success derives from creativity and innovation in addition to rigorous analysis. However, you cannot rigorously analyse the future; all you can do is rigorously analyse your creative and innovative view of it. The most sophisticated forms of extrapolation and trending from the past cannot yield such a view. You have to present your view (vision) first and then analyse it.

In other words, you cannot derive your vision from systematic analysis and a projection of trends. It must be your vision which forms the basis of analysis—not the other way around.

Expressed another way, you have to want to get somewhere. Having determined where you want to get to—your vision—you can then establish, by analysis, the feasibility of getting there and the best route.

A CHALLENGING AND INSPIRING VISION

Too many managers develop visions as if part of a training exercise, coming up with bland statements indistinguishable from other managers' bland statements. A vision, to be meaningful, must genuinely reflect your deep-rooted ambitions for the business. It must be challenging and inspiring. It must be a statement of where you want to take the business, whether it be in a slightly different direction or further expansion in the current direction.

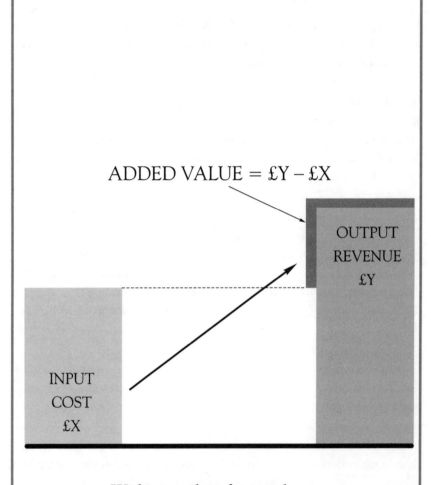

ADDED VALUE = £Y − £X

OUTPUT
REVENUE
£Y

INPUT
COST
£X

Without a clear financial
quantification of added value your
business plan becomes meaningless

FIGURE 3.9

The vision must be backed up by a personal set of beliefs about how you see the business and what it stands for, or should stand for.

Just look around you at the successful businesses of today and you will find that they stand apart from the competition in the way they reflect a clear set of beliefs, and in the practical and visionary way they have directed their business.

Business planning forces you to articulate clearly your own personal vision for the business and the beliefs you have about it. If this does not show through, the business plan will appear weak and come across as the product of a mechanical text-book exercise.

HEART AND MIND

There is, however, a counterbalancing factor. Your business plan cannot rely solely on vision and belief, no matter how much passion, drive, enthusiasm and confidence you have about the future success of your business. Too many managers get carried away with their visions and beliefs, neglecting to substantiate them. The heart has to be balanced by the mind (and vice versa). In the same way your passionate visions and beliefs have to be balanced by rigorous analysis to convince the powers that be that the vision can be achieved. Without such rigorous analysis the vision becomes merely a rather glib declaration of meaningless intent, or a kind of paradise fantasy. Merely stating that you intend to put a man on the moon is not enough. This vision has to be driven by a belief that it is possible and this belief has to be substantiated by a rigorous assessment of the feasibility of achieving it, as well as an outline route for getting there.

Rigorous analysis is essential for your business plan, but it must derive from your vision and beliefs about the future of your business.

OUTPUTS AND INPUTS

Business is all about delivering 'outputs' of higher value than the costs of the 'inputs' required to produce them.

NOTIONAL FIGURES

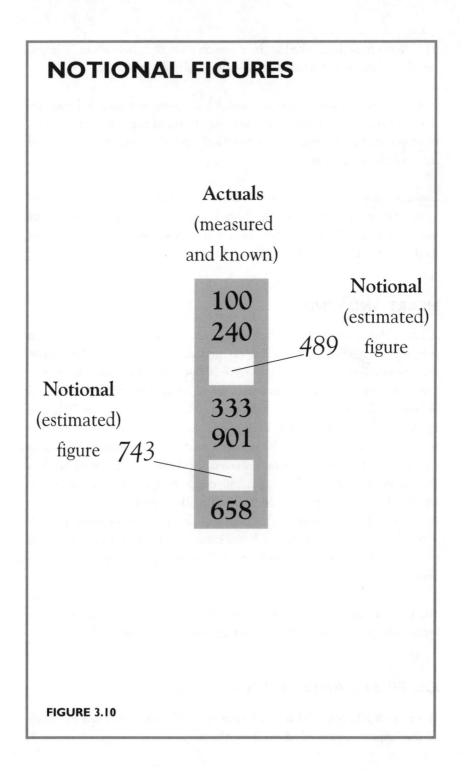

Actuals
(measured
and known)

Notional
(estimated)
figure

100
240

489

333
901

Notional
(estimated)
figure 743

658

FIGURE 3.10

The core of any business plan should, therefore, be a clear financial quantification of 'outputs' and 'inputs' and the 'added value' difference (see Fig. 3.9). Without this the business plan becomes meaningless.

The key is quantification. Too many so-called business plans produced by managers in large organizations are mere declarations of what they intend to do with the budgets they have bid for. There is little attempt to convert these declarations of intent into measurable outputs.

Yet any external business has to rely on producing and selling specified outputs quantified in terms of volume and price. Such outputs can be tangible goods produced or services defined by hours or days of time, projects completed, problems solved or tasks undertaken.

The biggest challenge for any manager who does not own his or her own business is to define the outputs and inputs (and, therefore, added value) for that part of the organization he or she works for.

The concept of 'notionality' is important here. Invariably a manager in a large organization will find that not all the information is available to quantify outputs and inputs. This can be overcome by inventing notional figures which are the manager's best estimate of what the real figures would be, if they were known. Often the use of notional figures to determine outputs and inputs forces a situation where the real figures soon become available.

The critical importance of defining ouputs and inputs and 'added value' is stressed throughout this book. In fact a clear definition of outputs and inputs should be at the core of your business plan and a key to it.

CREDIBILITY AND RISK

Business is synonymous with risk. If there was such a thing as a no-risk business we would all be millionaires.

This is why a reliance on scientific studies of business and management will never guarantee success. Scientific study of business attempts to

THE RISK FACTOR

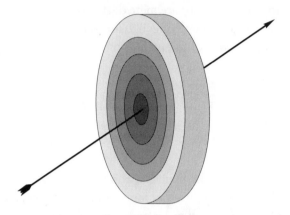

IDENTIFY RISKS

What if:

◆ the market fails to respond?
◆ the market over-responds?
◆ strikes are called?
◆ exchange rates fluctuate?
◆ interest rates go up?

ASSESS THE PROBABILITY
OF THE RISK OCCURRING

FIGURE 3.11

reduce it to a set of formulae, logics and rationales which (in theory) if applied will lead to success.

If there are any lessons to be learnt from such study they are about the application of creativity, intuition, innovation, common sense, 'gut-feel' and sheer determination as essential prerequisites for business success. Such factors inevitably include a large element of risk.

The key is to identify the risk in your business plan and to assess the potential negative impact of that risk occurring. What will happen if the market fails to respond to your planned initiative? What happens if it goes the other way and there is an overwhelming demand for your products, consequently overstretching limited capacity? What will be the impact on your business of varying exchange rates, or interest rates, or a competitor launching a comparable product?

Exposure of risk in your business plan does not mean frightening off your intended readers. More properly, it is aimed at establishing credibility by reassuring readers that you have assessed the risks you plan to take and the consequences of those risks occurring.

CRITICAL FACTORS

To assess risk you need to establish the critical factors on which your business is dependent. These may be the technical or professional exper-tise of key people, or an unrivalled distribution network, or a compre-hensive and up-to-date base of essential data. Essentially these critical factors are what makes your business unique. The risk is that your business suddenly ceases to be unique.

Credibility, however, is not just a matter of identifying and assessing risk. It is also about being internally consistent as well as being authoritative. Expressed another way, you need to know what you are talking about. The figures in the plan have to add up and any statement you make needs to be substantiated.

The business plan has to prove to your readers that the overall risk of backing you is worth taking. Not only do you have to establish your

TARGETED STYLE

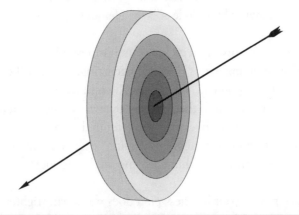

TARGET

◆ Who are my readers?

◆ How do I best capture their attention?

◆ How do I best present my plan?

◆ How do I best get my points across?

◆ How much information should I give?

◆ How do I best obtain their approval?

FIGURE 3.12

credentials (by demonstrating your track record) but you also have to show that you have a rare combination of shrewd judgement and entrepreneurial flair.

Thus your business plan has to be incredibly persuasive.

There is a secret to convincing your readers in this way—first convince yourself!

Try to imagine persuading one of your readers to stake his or her livelihood on the successful implementation of your business plan. Try to imagine convincing one of your readers to risk millions of pounds of his or her own money supporting you. Assume your readers have a choice as to whether to back you and your business or someone else. Why should they choose you?

Unless you can work through these scenarios and answer these questions you will not have a credible business plan.

TARGETED STYLE

Your plan is a work of art.

The way in which you present your plan is as critical as the substance it contains. This does not necessarily mean glossy productions with neat artwork and alluring colours.

It means you have to capture your readers' imagination with the words you use. It means that in addition to letting the facts speak for themselves (by being clearly presented), you have to express yourself in a way that sparks your readers' interest. And your readers will vary depending on the industry you are in and their own personal background.

If you are a civil servant whose operation is being market tested you will need to pitch your plan in a totally different way from a caterer planning to open a short chain of restaurants.

STRATEGY—A DEFINITION

Strategy is the art of creating value. It provides the intellectual frameworks, conceptual models, and governing ideas that allow a company's managers to identify opportunities for bringing value to customers and for delivering that value at a profit.

In this respect, strategy is the way a company defines its business and links together the only two resources that really matter in today's economy: knowledge and relationships or an organization's competencies and customers.

Richard Normann and Rafael Ramírez,
Harvard Business Review July–August 1993

FIGURE 3.13

As will be discussed later, irrespective of your targeted style there are key qualities applicable to all plans—qualities like brevity and an easy to follow structure.

DISTILLATION TO THE BARE ESSENCE

Avoid being boring. Avoid attempting to snow your reader with masses of data. To be more idiomatic, 'cut the claptrap'. Try to distil your thoughts and analysis down to the bare essence, using support appendices where appropriate.

In developing your style think carefully about every word you use. Consider every section and how it fits into the overall structure. Think carefully about how you illustrate each key point.

More importantly, ensure your plan is self-contained. Use language that your reader will understand (which is not necessarily the one you use at work). Avoid acronyms, jargon and in-house terms.

While your enthusiasm for your plan must show through, balance it with clearly demonstrated business judgement. Differentiate opinion from fact.

Writing is an art form. Enjoy the experience. The creativity of your business plan is not only in the futuristic ideas you are presenting but in the imaginative way you present those ideas, allowing the reader to focus clearly on them.

You will have to make a judgement about the quality of the printing, binding and layout. Poor typing and substandard copying will undoubtedly undermine your plan. Conversely, too much gloss can repel your reader. Your plan should look good but not spectacular.

The style of your business plan is all about crafting a clear articulation of your ideas for the future.

◆ indestructible

◆ fireproof

◆ flawless

◆ accurate

◆ factually correct

FIGURE 3.14

INDESTRUCTIBILITY

Your plan should be fireproof—virtually indestructible.

There are always people around who delight in finding flaws in others' arguments. One of your readers will be such a person. These people serve a valuable purpose. If your plan has flaws they deserve to be exposed. Why risk substantial sums of money on flawed argument?

Be clear, however, that it *is* a flaw not to identify and expose a risk! You will have failed if one of your readers exposes it for you.

Every component part of your business plan should, therefore, be fully tested. Even if you have to use notional figures, it is not difficult to test them against real ones which you have researched out.

Some simple rules apply:

◆ Never make statements which cannot easily be substantiated

◆ Never confuse opinion with fact

◆ Justify your assertions clearly

◆ Avoid manipulating the statistics (everyone else will know the game)

◆ Be enthusiastic but do not exaggerate

◆ Base your plan on 'the worst possible case' (minimum sales, highest costs) although you may wish to present additionally 'the best possible case' (maximum sales, lowest costs) as well

◆ Get your facts right

◆ Be accurate

◆ Make sure your sums add up

FORECASTING AND PLANNING—THE DIFFERENCE

Like the weather, business is a chaotic system in which small differences in the starting point can translate into large divergences in the final outcome.

To say that we cannot forecast where our organizations will be in five years' time is not to say that we cannot plan for the future.

John Kay, *Foundations of Corporate Success* Oxford 1992

In 1971 *Time* magazine published the dire predictions of the Club of Rome, a panel of 70 experts who announced that the world was running out of oil and that we had only about 40 years' worth left, or about 700 billion barrels. However, 20 years later— when we should have had only 500 billion barrels remaining—we discovered that we still had 900 billion barrels!

From an article by Anthony Robbins, *Business Age* September 1993

FIGURE 3.15

◆ Spell out your assumptions clearly

Step 4 of the business planning process is to put your plan to the test and the recommended process for this is outlined in Chapter 8.

By the time you submit the finished plan to your intended readers you should be in a position to defend the plan from attack from any quarter. And some people will want to attack you.

So, be prepared. Ensure your plan is indestructible!

TARGET READERS OF PLAN	PURPOSE OF PLAN
Yourself	◆ To clarify your own thinking about the future ◆ To produce a clear focus for monitoring and controlling future progress
Your team	◆ To involve your team in determining the future direction of the business and thus to secure their commitment and motivation
External funders (Bankers, venture capitalists, etc.)	◆ To put up a convincing case to secure external funding for the future development of the business
Internal funders (Senior executives, finance department, *etc.*)	◆ To present a clear 'business case' to persuade senior executives to support your proposal for developing the business unit for which you are responsible
Shareholders/owners/ trustees/boards/ governors/ politicians, etc. (public services)	◆ To reinforce the confidence of shareholders, owners (or politicians, etc., if you are in public services) that you have the capability to manage successfully your business in the future

FIGURE 4.1

PRELIMINARY STEP— DETERMINING THE PURPOSE OF YOUR BUSINESS PLAN

> ❛Lay plans for the accomplishment of the difficult before it becomes difficult; make something big by starting with it when small.❜
>
> Lao Tzu *Tao te Ching*

Before engaging in any work on your plan you should first determine its purpose and who you are aiming it at.

In other words, what are you seeking to achieve with the plan? There are a range of options, one or more of which might apply (see Fig. 4.1).

At every stage of the business planning process you should be conscious of the impact any decision you want to make will have on the readers of the plan.

Your plan should, therefore, always be focused on your audience. To achieve this try to put yourself in your readers' shoes; try to think how they might react to each statement you are making. What impression would you have if you were a banker, or a senior boss reading this plan?

Think of all the plans, reports and papers you have read in the past. What are the qualities that make an excellent plan stand out from a poor one?

Should you be seeking approval of your plan, try to think of the criteria the 'approver' will be using in evaluating the plan. Will it just be the bottom line figures or something more?

PRELIMINARY STEP CHECKLIST

My plan is aimed at the following people:	I want to achieve the following as a result of these people reading my plan:

FIGURE 4.2

Many bankers when confronted with a business plan confess to going straight to the appendices at the back to look at the bottom line projections and cash flows. Others confess to ignoring all the 'blurb' and being put off by too much gloss. They will be more impressed by the 'content' than by fancy covers and arty photographs.

Having undertaken this preliminary step of determining the purpose of the plan and its intended readership, you will find it easier to present the final version in a clear, succinct and easily accessible way.

As you go through the business planning process, therefore, continually ask yourself:

◆ 'How am I going to present this in the plan?'

◆ 'How is this going to tie together with everything else?'

◆ 'How does this relate to the position from which my potential "approver" will be coming?'

◆ 'What will my readers be looking for in the plan?'

In other words, 'What am I really seeking to achieve with this plan?'

Figure 4.2 opposite provides a simple checklist to help you with this preliminary step.

DEFINING YOUR BUSINESS— INITIAL EXERCISE

Imagine that you arrive next Monday morning to discover that your existing boss has moved on and your employer has appointed a new boss. This new boss has asked you for a ten-minute presentation about the business unit you run.

What are the key characteristics you are going to refer to in describing your business? List them in the following table.

Key characteristics of your business

FIGURE 5.1

STEP I—DEFINING YOUR BUSINESS

❢The secret of business is to know something that nobody else knows.❢

Aristotle Onassis

To be credible a business plan must be based on current reality. The essential first step to the business planning process, therefore, is to define your business as it now exists. This chapter provides a guide to this process of definition.

In an ideal world you would know your own business inside out. The danger is that in the real world you delude yourself into thinking you know all about your business—when in fact you do not.

UNIQUENESS

The concept of uniqueness is important here. Your business cannot survive and thrive unless there is something unique about it. That uniqueness needs to be evident in every aspect of the business plan and especially in the definition of the business as it currently exists.

Undertake the exercise opposite (Fig. 5.1) as a preliminary step to defining your business. It will help you to identify the key characteristics of the unit for which you are responsible.

THE BASICS

It is surprising that many 'business managers' are not clear about some of the basics of their business. For example, some do not even know who their customers are or what markets they are in.

BUSINESS BASICS

◆ Who are our customers?

◆ What are our products?

◆ What are our services?

◆ Who are our suppliers?

◆ What are our assets?

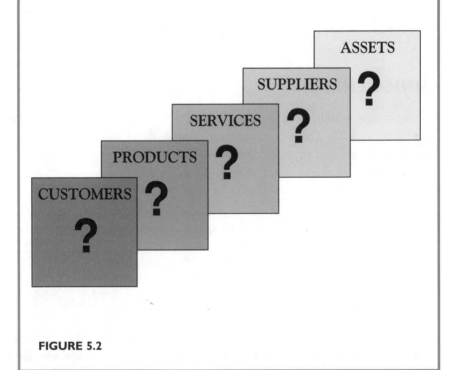

FIGURE 5.2

THE SUCCESSFUL MANAGER'S GUIDE TO BUSINESS PLANNING

If you supply computer equipment, for example, are your customers:

◆ end-users (people who use the terminals)?

◆ their managers?

◆ the purchasing department (the procurers)?

◆ the directors of the company?

◆ the dealers who sell to the company?

It is not good enough to say 'Our customer is Company A'. Customers are people, and you have to be clear who you are selling to and serving.

The same question also applies to defining internal customers. For example, if you are managing the finance department for a large company, are your customers:

◆ the main board directors who have accountability for the financial well-being of the company?

◆ the shareholders or owners (or politicians, governors, trustees if you are a public sector organization)?

◆ line managers who need financial information and advice in order to monitor and control their own area of business responsibility?

Furthermore, in managing your business you will need to be 100 per cent clear about the products and services ('outputs') you are responsible for selling and supplying.

If your business unit is a training function, for instance, what are your products and services? Are they:

◆ the delivery of *all* technical training products to *all* departments?

◆ the delivery of *specific* technical training to *specific* departments?

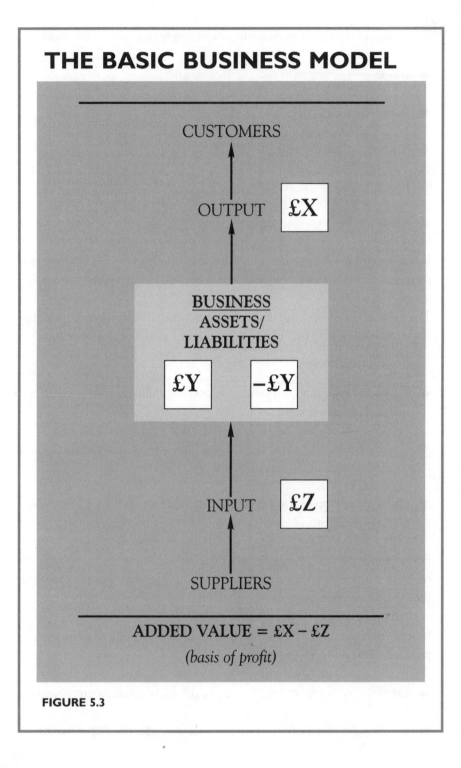

THE BASIC BUSINESS MODEL

CUSTOMERS

OUTPUT £X

BUSINESS
ASSETS/
LIABILITIES

£Y   −£Y

INPUT £Z

SUPPLIERS

ADDED VALUE = £X − £Z

(basis of profit)

FIGURE 5.3

- the delivery of all (or some) forms of management training?

- the provision of consultancy advice on training to all departments?

- the provision of consultancy advice on all aspects of organization and personal development?

- the arranging (broking) of training—i.e. procuring training resources on behalf of departments

In too many large organizations managers are unclear about these basic questions, often because they operate in a purely reactionary mode. When you run your own business you need to be very clear about the products and services you supply and to which customers. This is an essential part of your 'business thinking'.

While many internal service managers allege they run their unit on a 'business footing', they often do not see themselves as having customers. Many of these managers (responsible for central functions) still see their role as exercising approval systems which control the operation of line departments. Finance, personnel and IT departments are particularly prone to a controlling preference (or interference).

THE BASIC BUSINESS MODEL

The first step in defining your business is, therefore, to envisage your area of responsibility (your business unit) in terms of a 'basic business model' (see Fig. 5.3). From this model you can develop a clear definition of your business and consequently plan for the future.

The model simply assumes that you manage a business comprising a number of defined assets and liabilities which are used to convert the supply of goods and services (inputs) into other goods and services (outputs) which are sold to customers. The difference between the cost of inputs supplied and the revenue earned from outputs sold is called 'added value' and forms the basis of your profit.

OUTPUTS

An output is:

◆ A unit of service (or product) delivered to a customer

For managers in large organizations an output is:

◆ What you would 'sell' if you were a private company
◆ What your customers (internal or external) would 'buy' from you

Examples of outputs:

★ *An hour of a professional's time*
★ *A training course*
★ *A project completed*
  (e.g. conveyancing on a house sale/purchase)
★ *A day of a professional's time*
★ *A year's supply of services*
  (e.g. a maintenance contract)
★ *A one-off job completed*
  (e.g. repair of an item)
★ *Processing 'x' number of documents*

FIGURE 5.4

Accountants will tell you it is a little more complicated than that. Actually it is not. It is simply a matter of realizing that everything to do with money in your business can be seen in terms of outputs and inputs (your profit and loss account) or in terms of assets and liabilities (your balance sheet). The flow of money, of course, is also important in terms of when you pay your suppliers and when your customers pay you. So you will need to see your business in terms of cash flow too.

The two key concepts in this basic business model are those of outputs and inputs.

OUTPUTS

A unit of output is a service or product delivered to a customer. If you run your own commercial business this is easily defined. The output can be a pair or shoes sold (or repaired) or the installation of a new central heating system. Or it can be the completion by a solicitor of the conveyancing required for the purchase of a house, or the handling of your annual tax return by your accountant.

The definition of output is more difficult for those managers who do not run their own business and manage an internal business unit in a large organization. In these cases a unit of output is what you **would** sell if you were a private company. It is what your customers (internal or external) would 'buy' from you (see Fig. 5.4). Thus if you are managing the company's internal 'central services' (for example the central typing pool, stationery stores and reprographics), you will need to imagine that you are running a high street operation selling these very same services. In the high street operation, a customer rings up and orders a ream of typing paper, or comes in with a 10 page report that has to be copied 20 times, or a dictation tape which has to be typed up as 14 separate letters. In each case, a charge for each of these units of product and service output would be put on the account of the customer who would then be billed at the end of the month.

If your area of responsibility is the company's internal 'central services' then you have to identify clearly the same types of output units if you are to

BEDFORDSHIRE COUNTY COUNCIL
Central Services
OUTPUTS (per year)

ACCOMMODATION SERVICES

Unlocking and locking of	
buildings (Weekdays)	5000
(Weekends)	50
Emergency call outs	48
Evening lettings (3 buildings)	310
Confidential waste collection	
and shredding (sacks)	8000
Car passes reissued	300
Security pass cards reissued	240
Office moves arranged	50
Cleaning variation orders	43
Cleaning inspections	2408
Caretaking hours	14 890

RECEPTION SERVICES (3 buildings)

No. fax messages received	21 934
No. of incoming calls	402 250
No. of visitors	48 576
No. of internal	
teledirectories issued	1
No. of room bookings made	2540

MAILROOM SERVICES

No. of postal items franked	338 820
No. of postal items received	412 500
No. of courier visits	18 500
No. of items handled by	
courier service	62 400
No. of parcels received	3000
No. of recorded and	
registered items received	1860
Ditto dispatched	1750

LAND CHARGES AND SEARCHES

No. of common searches	
completed	844
No. of land charges searches	
completed	12 397
No. of enquiries	127

ORDERS

No. of public inquiries attended	3
No. of rights of way orders	59
No. of highway orders	87
No. of private street work notices	30
No. of road hump notices	2
No. of advance payment code	
notices	16

MEMBER AND PROPER OFFICER
SERVICES

No. of chairman visits arranged	140
No. of charity, meals, special	
events arranged	19
No. of letters typed	881
No. of stationery orders placed	140
No. of meetings booked	720
No. of messages actioned, etc.	1375
No. of member vacancies filled	
(election)	74
No. of vacancies filled:	
Registration	13
Rent officer	4
Coroner	0
No. of complaints handled:	
Registration	34
Rent officer	1
Coroner	1
No. of queries/problems processed:	
Registration	1820
Rent officer	23
Coroner	7

*Extracted with permission from the Central Services Business Plan
of Bedfordshire County Council*

FIGURE 5.5

manage in a businesslike way and produce a business plan. An example of a Departmental approach to outputs is shown opposite (see Fig. 5.5).

Furthermore, you have to be very clear about your inputs.

INPUTS

An input is a unit of cost incurred in delivering a service or product. Effectively it is the cost of what you need to buy in to provide the services (or outputs) you deliver. It is the cost of what you obtain from your suppliers—whether they be external or internal (see Fig. 5.6 overleaf).

External inputs include everything from stationery to the use of subcontractors or casual staff. Internal inputs include the cost of paying your staff as well as overheads such as rent and related charges.

Without clearly defined and quantified outputs and inputs, it is impossible to think in a businesslike way or produce a meaningful business plan. But not **totally** impossible! You should not be defeated if you cannot immediately quantify all those inputs wrapped up in global overheads. The secret is to insert into your business plan, as already stated, notional figures based on the best approximations you can make to the real figures.

On the following pages (Figs 5.7 and 5.8) is a hypothetical example of how the work of a senior administrator can be translated into inputs and outputs. If you were running your business you would only take on a senior administrator costing £32 000 per year if you were clear about the productive outputs this person would deliver and the effective revenue this person would bring in.

In defining your business in terms of outputs and inputs it is important to see every member of your staff as a supplier providing an input to achieve an output in the way illustrated by the example of J. Smith, senior administrator. Using this example go through the same thought process of each person for whom you are responsible, whether that person is a secretary, clerk, production operator, receptionist, personnel officer, inspector, member of the typing pool, internal consultant, sales person or planner.

INPUTS

An input is:

◆ A unit of cost incurred in providing a service (product delivery)

For managers in large organizations an input is:

◆ The cost of what you need to 'buy in' to provide the services you deliver

◆ The cost of what you 'obtain' from your suppliers (external and internal—including staff)

Examples of inputs:

★ *An hour/day/month/year of your staff's time*

★ *A training course for a member of your staff*

★ *Stationery*

★ *Rent and related charges (electricity, etc.)*

★ *Telephones*

★ *Other overheads*

FIGURE 5.6

AN EXAMPLE OF INPUT

J. Smith

Senior

Administrator

200 work-days p.a.

£20 000 salary
+ £12 000 on costs
(+ overheads)

£160 (+) per day

£20 (+) per hour

◆ What do you get for an INPUT of 200 work-days from J. Smith?

◆ What do you get for an INPUT costing £32 000 (+ overheads)?

◆ As a result of this INPUT:

What service is delivered?

What is the work done?

What is the value added?

What would NOT happen if the work was not done?

THE ANSWER IS - - - - ->>>>

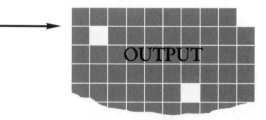

OUTPUT

(INPUT *MUST* LEAD TO OUTPUT)

FIGURE 5.7

AN EXAMPLE OF OUTPUT

Input:	200 work-days
	£20 000 salary
Senior	+ £12 000 on costs
Administrator	(+ overheads)
	£160 (+) per day
J. Smith	£20 (+) per hour

What is the OUTPUT for a typical 40 days' INPUT?

| 20 DAYS' OUTPUT ('revenue earning') | 50% | PRODUCTIVE OUTPUT |

6 days processing procedure X for Dept. Y

5 days processing procedure A for Dept. B

4 days developing System G for Dept. H

5 days giving advice to Dept. M

- -

5 days on training

6 days at team meetings

9 days managing staff

| NON-PRODUCTIVE TIME | 50% | 20 SUPPORT DAYS ('non-revenue earning') |

Output Cost = £40/hour + overhead + profit = **PRICE/HOUR**

FIGURE 5.8

All the time try to imagine that your area of responsibility is a self-contained business with discrete suppliers and customers. Keep on asking yourself such basic questions as:

◆ How much does it cost me to have the windows in my office cleaned (or should I negotiate an overall contract for all cleaning services)?

◆ How much does it cost me for the maintenance of the computer systems my team and I use?

◆ How much do I pay for the accountancy and financial advice I get?

◆ What is my telephone bill?

There are many other questions like this—questions which, if you were running a self-contained business, you would know the answers to. If you are an internal business manager you also need the same answers, otherwise these costs will get out of control. You will be responsible for outputs and someone else (normally in the centre) will be responsible for costs such as window cleaning, general cleaning, financial advice and telephone bills.

DEALING WITH CENTRAL CHARGES

If your organization is encouraging you to think in a 'businesslike' way, for example, by preparing a business plan, the issue of central charges (or overheads) is critical. Too many old-fashioned traditional hierarchical organizations simply 'dump' an allocation of these central charges on line departments. This is often done without explanation or negotiation and with no real attempt to measure the effectiveness of the service provision represented by these charges. In a real-life business situation the imposition of exhorbitant levels of overheads would render the business uncompetitive. They must, therefore, be challenged until the recipient of the central service feels that he or she is getting value for money. Conflicts will arise as soon as the recipient feels that a more effective service could be obtained more cheaply by using external suppliers.

No business can operate satisfactorily when being dumped upon from above.

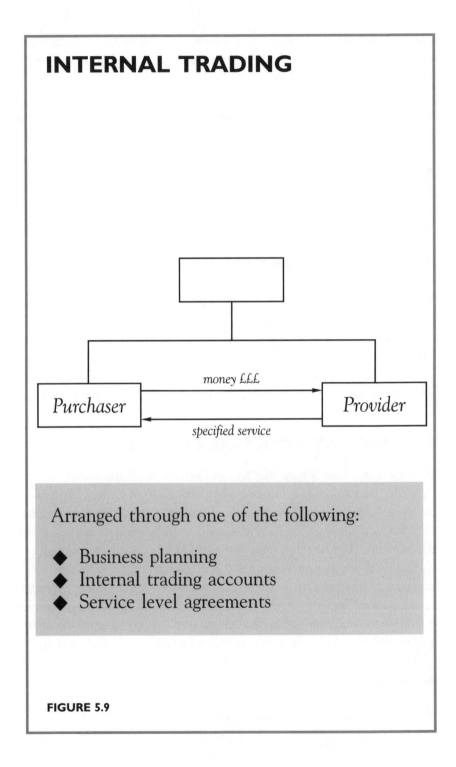

INTERNAL TRADING

| Purchaser | money £££ ⟶ | Provider |

specified service

Arranged through one of the following:

◆ Business planning
◆ Internal trading accounts
◆ Service level agreements

FIGURE 5.9

INTERNAL TRADING

The progressive trend is to devolve service budgets to line units who then purchase those services from the centre. This gives more discretion over the use of internal services to managers of business units and enables them to simulate a trading situation, accounting for the services they use, whereas before the costs of such service had been 'lost' in central charges. Devolvement thus forces central functions to 'stand up and be counted' for the provision of cost-effective and valued services to internal customers. In such organizations, the customers (line units) are no longer forced to use, for example, central personnel but actually purchase a service from them (as if they were an external supplier). This process can be facilitated through the use of 'service level agreements' or 'internal trading accounts' or through the use of business plans which specify the volume, type and quality of services to be delivered to Business Unit A by Business Unit B.

While the concept of internal trading has the main attraction of encouraging managers to think in a businesslike way, it does suffer from the danger of over-bureaucratization as managers attempt to measure and charge for every minor interaction between two business units. This danger can be averted by applying a common sense approach which simulates real-life business situations. For example, if you were running your own business would you really charge a major customer for an extra half-hour of your time, or for giving them a complimentary copy of a report?

In the real world of business not all work is chargeable as an output delivered to a customer. There will always be a fair degree of 'development' type work where there is contact with the customer but no chargeable output. Time spent prospecting for sales obviously falls into this category, as does time invested in developing a good relationship with a customer. A business judgement therefore has to be made between chargeable time and non-chargeable time. Normally it would not be cost-effective to measure and charge for all the minor transactions and interactions that take place between two business units. Such transactions should, therefore, be swept into non-chargeable time. Only clearly-defined and specified outputs should be charged for. Any attempt to do otherwise

DEFINE YOUR BUSINESS— CHECKLIST

An initial definition

Name the business		
Main activity of business		
List your main customers		
State the markets you are currently working in (indicate also approximate % share of market)		
Name your main competitors		
Identify your key units of output		
Specify the key assets and liabilities		
Identify your key units of input		
List your main suppliers		

FIGURE 5.10

will simply alienate the customer who will think he or she is being over-charged.

The big test for large organizations attempting to introduce business planning is, therefore, to break down central charges into discrete and measurable components related to clearly-defined and specified services or outputs. If you are an internal business manager you are going to need a lot of courage and conviction to challenge your organization to do this, if they are not doing so already.

Too many organizations exhort their managers to think and act in a businesslike way and then tie their hands behind their backs by insisting they use unspecified central services at prohibitive charges which are simply imposed upon them. When this happens, business planning becomes a charade.

A clear definition of outputs and inputs is, therefore, central to the whole business planning process.

Having defined the outputs and inputs of your current business you will need to extend the definition to give a complete picture. Figure 5.10 provides a checklist to help you with this while, over the page, Fig. 5.11 provides an indication of what should be included on the checklist.

It is vitally important that the readers of your plan are clear not only about your business's outputs and inputs but also about who its customers are, the market it is in, its competitors, its assets and liabilities, and its suppliers.

DEFINING YOUR BUSINESS— CHECKLIST/EXAMPLES

Customers	External (e.g. chief executive company A) Internal (e.g. personnel director)
Market	External (e.g. government agencies) Internal (e.g. all line departments)
Competitors	External (e.g. local consultancies) Internal (e.g. management services)
Outputs (products)	One hour of service Completion of assignment/project
Assets/ liabilities	Unique product/brand name Property/plant /equipment, etc. Goodwill/intellectual property Cash in hand/debts, etc.
Inputs	Professional advice Consumables Administration
Suppliers	External (e.g. consultancy X) Internal (e.g. finance department)

NB: This list is not intended to be either
exhaustive or comprehensive

FIGURE 5.11

HISTORICAL QUANTIFICATION

You will now have to take the broad definition of your business and quantify it. Again if you run your own business your annual accounts for the last three years will provide the base data for this, to which may be added any other, more detailed, management accounts that you maintain.

If you do not have available a set of current and historical accounts, it is important that you attempt to produce such a set, or some form of quantification of how your business unit has performed over recent years. No one is going to believe your projections about the future unless they can compare them with your current and past performance. Quantification is essential during this process. Use notional figures where appropriate.

Figure 5.12, over the page, gives a simple example of how you might build up a definition of quantified outputs (revenue) and inputs (costs) for a small team of professional people. The bottom line, of course, is the difference between the revenue and the costs—in other words, the added value from which you derive your profit figure. Your accountant will need to make some adjustments for factors such as depreciation and to adjust this initial 'bottom line' to determine the real level of profit.

Figure 5.13, on page 78 provides a template for building up a historical quantification of your business. The best way of doing this is to use the spreadsheet facility on your computer. You can then adapt and amend as you build up the picture. Even so, a manual system can prove fairly quick if you can invest some time developing a template along the lines shown.

There are a number of essential documents you will require to support your business plan. The summary accounts for the last three years have already been mentioned. In addition, you will need your most recent annual report, examples of sales and product literature, together with an organization chart for your business.

Furthermore, it is important that you have career resumés for each member of your team.

SMALL PROFESSIONAL UNIT

No.	Description (Salary + on-cost)	Total cost (Salaries + on-costs) £		Productive days (Actual/ available)	Productive Time%	Day Rate £	Revenue £
Staff inputs				**Outputs**			
1	Unit Manager	100 000		80/200	40	1000	80 000
5	Senior staff (£70 000)	350 000		600/1000	60	800	480 000
10	Junior staff (£40 000)	400 000		1600/2000	80	500	800 000
5	Support staff (£16 000)	80 000		900/1000	90	200	18 000
	Expenses recharged	60 000					60 000
	Total (staff input costs: A)	**990 000**					

Sale of 100 reports at £100 each	10 000
Sale of 10 two-day training courses at £3000 each	30 000
TOTAL OUTPUT REVENUE	**1 478 000**

Other inputs

Printing, postage, stationery	60 000
Telephones	30 000
Rent (2500 sq. ft at £12/sq. ft)	30 000
Service charges (to landlord)	9000
Office cleaning	8000
Advertising, PR support	12 000
Legal advice	5000
Accountants' fee, audit	12 000
Training, conferences	14 000
Non-rechargeable travel, etc.	24 000
Casual staff	8000
Computer maintenance	9000
Entertainment	13 000
Recruitment expenses	4000
Bank charges	6000
Insurance	3000
Total (other inputs: B)	**247 000**
Total inputs: A + B	**1 237 000**

FIGURE 5.12

It is also helpful to have to hand your current mission statement together with any documents relating to your management approach and organizational philosophy. Finally, copies of any press cuttings about your business can provide useful backup.

At this stage you should prepare a list of additional data and documentation you will need to collect to help you complete your definition of the business. While your business plan will provide an overview of the business as it is now (and has been over the last few years), it is important that each statement within it can be substantiated by hard fact. The data and documentation you collect will provide the backup for this (see Fig. 5.14 on page 79).

You will also need to spell out your achievements over the last three years. It may be wise to sit down with your team and with your own boss to review these. These achievements are part of your track record (the other part being the quantification of performance referred to above).

Coupled with this is an open and honest statement about the strengths and weaknesses of your current business. Again your team and your boss can help you with this.

In portraying your achievements and strengths do not be modest! One of the reasons for having a business plan is to convince other people of your ability to take the business forward. To that extent you must be prepared to sell yourself as well as the rest of your team, highlighting all your accomplishments and good points. However, such a plan would not be credible unless you are honest enough to admit the lessons of the past together with current deficiencies and weaknesses which you intend to address. These weaknesses should include any constraints you see being imposed upon the business.

It is worth repeating that nobody is going to support you in pursuit of your planned future achievements unless you can readily portray achievements to date. Examples of achievements, and strengths and weaknesses are given in Fig. 5.15 on page 81.

HISTORICAL QUANTIFICATION— QUANTIFY YOUR INPUTS AND OUTPUTS

Historical analysis– your track record		Measure (units)	Two years ago No. of units	Last year No. of units	This year No. of units	Revenue–income Two years ago £	Last year £	This year £
OUTPUTS	e.g. Consultancy	Days	200	220	280	80 000	132 000	150 000
(units 'sold' and revenue income)								
TOTAL OUTPUTS								
INPUTS	e.g. Advice from finance	Hours	300	340	400	COSTS 18 000	23 000	30 000
(units 'bought' and unit costs)								
TOTAL INPUTS								

FIGURE 5.13

Having collated all this documentation and data, together with a clear quantification of your outputs and inputs over the last three years, you are now in a position to write the two chapters in your business plan which outline your current business and your past performance. The process for writing this will be covered in Chapter 9, **Step 5**.

ADDITIONAL DATA AND DOCUMENTS

	List here the additional data you need to obtain
EXAMPLES	
Data and documents relating to:	
◆ Inputs	
◆ Input units (measures)	
◆ Outputs	
◆ Output units (measures)	
◆ Historic data	
◆ Input unit costs	
◆ Output charges	
◆ Products	
◆ Services	
◆ Customers	
◆ Suppliers	
◆ Competitors	
◆ Pricing data	
◆ Financial data	
◆ Assets	
◆ Liabilities	
◆ Staffing levels	
◆ Organization charts	
◆ Publicity	
◆ Key ratios	
◆ Summary accounts	
◆ Sales literature	
◆ Product literature	

FIGURE 5.14

ACHIEVEMENTS (your track record):
identify the main achievements in your business over the last two years. Examples are listed below.

◆ Average queue times reduced from 12 to 4 minutes by reorganization of reception
◆ Absenteeism reduced from 8% to 2% with staff involvement programme
◆ 10% increase in work (output) due to development of new specialism
◆ Revenue from sale of specialist reports increased from £10 000 to £26 000
◆ Attracted 10 major new customers to our service while only losing one
◆ Extended opening hours from 9.00 a.m.–5.00 p.m. to 8.30 a.m.– 5.30 p.m.
◆ Reduced wastage from 4% to 1%
◆ Gained major publicity coverage for our new service
◆ Introduced 'money back' guarantee with very positive results
◆ Market survey shows we have developed a reputation as leaders in our field
◆ Major investment in training programme led to significant rise in quality standards
◆ Have beaten financial targets for each of last three years
◆ Have retained stable and experienced management team

STRENGTHS AND WEAKNESSES:
identify the current strengths and weaknesses of your business. Examples are listed below.

Strengths
◆ Expertize/experience/track record of senior management team
◆ Extensive network of customers across region
◆ Database profiling market
◆ Faster response to customer needs than most competitors
◆ Positive attitudes of all staff
◆ High reputation in market-place

Weaknesses
◆ Lack of business training for many staff
◆ Cramped premises/unsuitable location
◆ A small number of unreliable suppliers
◆ Insufficient time to develop business
◆ Some products are ageing, need replacement
◆ Slowness in responding to competitive pressures
◆ Not developing sufficient talent on front-line

FIGURE 5.15

'MIRACLES OF MARKETING—HOW TO REINVENT YOUR PRODUCT' by Ingrid Abramovitch (an extract)

Until 1982 Howard Schultz was based in New York as VP of US operations for the Swedish housewares company Hammarplast. That year he was asked to move to Seattle to join Starbucks, a coffee retailing company, to manage retail sales and marketing.

He and his wife, Sheri Kersch-Schultz, packed their belongings and drove 3000 miles west to Seattle.

About a year later, Schultz visited Italy on a buying trip. As he wandered through the piazzas of Milan, he was overcome with a vision. 'I saw the relationship Italian culture has with coffee and the romance of the beverage,' he says. 'The Italian starts his day at the coffee bar and sees his friends there later on. It struck me that this was also possible in America. It had never been done—and we could do it because the quality of Starbucks coffee is unsurpassed.'

Schultz became obsessed. He was determined to build a national chain of Starbucks cafés based on the Italian coffee bar, but his bosses were reluctant.

Frustrated, Schultz left Starbucks and wrote a business plan for a new company. He returned to Italy to visit hundreds of coffee bars and document his findings on videotape.

Schultz approached 242 potential investors. After a year, he managed to raise $1.7 million. In April 1986, Schultz opened his first coffee bar and

called it Il Giornale, after the Italian newspaper, and served Starbucks coffee. It was an immediate success. Schultz soon opened another in Seattle and a third in Vancouver.

A year later he bought out his old bosses at Starbucks for about $4 million and in August 1987 Schultz dropped the name Il Giornale and merged his stores with Starbucks.

In 1992 the company went public with a stock price of $17 which subsequently climbed to $40. In early January 1993, Schultz gathered his top managers to officially announce the first-quarter results for fiscal year 1993. The results were Starbucks' best to date: Sales were up 72 per cent in the first quarter to $38.6 million, and profits leapt 101 per cent.

From the start, Schultz built his business around cautious growth. His first move, after a careful audit of his newly acquired company, was to write a new business plan. He laid out a vision—one he has faithfully adhered to ever since.

Starbucks would become the leading North American retailer of speciality coffee. Starbucks would grow carefully, entering one city at a time and dominating the market before moving on to the next.

First appeared in SUCCESS, April 1993
Written by Ingrid Abramovitch
Reprinted with permission of SUCCESS Magazine
Copyright 1993 by HAL HOLDINGS, INC.

FIGURE 6.1

STEP 2—FUTURE THINKING

6

❛*You can never plan the future by the past.*❜
Edmund Burke 1729–1797

This chapter suggests an approach for stimulating your future think-ing about your business. The next three steps are the essential core of the business planning process and focus on the future direction of your business.

Step 2, which is dealt with in this chapter, concentrates on eliciting your view (or vision) about the future of your business and translating this into priority strategic objectives. In turn these priority strategic objectives have to be converted into quantitative projections. Chapter 7 (**Step 3**) addresses this. Finally your concepts, strategic objectives and projections will need to be challenged using a rigorous testing process. Chapter 8 (**Step 4**) deals with this.

The first of these steps (**Step 2**) can prove perhaps to be the most exhilarating aspect of business planning. It is best conducted with your immediate team. Their commitment to a future vision of your business and the priority strategic objectives is essential. An example of the visionary approach of an American company, Starbucks, is given oppo-site (see Fig. 6.1).

Step 2 is all about developing and confirming a vision which reveals how you and your team see the future of the business. The critical term here is uniqueness. The picture you develop of your future business must clearly differentiate it from any other business. Without such differentiation you cannot be successful. Additionally, this vision (of uniqueness) must be

EXERCISE YOUR VISION

IT IS THREE YEARS ON FROM TODAY

Imagine in your own mind that it is three years on from today. You and your team have been incredibly successful in achieving the vision you established for your business at the three day workshop at the XYZ Hotel three years ago.

What exactly has been achieved? Brainstorm out your visionary ideas in relation to:

PRODUCT DEVELOPMENT	SALES AND MARKETING	ORGANIZATION, MANAGEMENT AND PEOPLE

INFORMATION
AND ADMINISTRATION

TECHNOLOGY

OVERALL BUSINESS
RESULTS

Summarize your answers on Fig. 6.3

FIGURE 6.2

underpinned by a clear statement which echoes what the business is all about and what you stand for in managing it.

These will be your values and beliefs in relation to your business and as such will be inextricably linked to your vision.

FACILITATION

The most effective way of undertaking this initial 'future-thinking' process is to locate some distant hotel in a tranquil setting and lock yourself and your team away for around three days.

Many teams prefer to use the services of an external facilitator for this process. While the best facilitators may prove incredibly expensive, they do have the virtue of being independent and able to challenge you and the team in a very positive and constructive way. An excellent facilitator will be able to free up your thinking to explore the unlimited opportunities which continually pass your business by.

Furthermore, an independent facilitator will free you from the bind of having to chair a team meeting at the same time as having to assert your views about the future.

BRAINSTORM THE FUTURE

During your first session at the hotel break your team into small groups and ask them to brainstorm out a picture (vision) of how they see the business in two, three (or even five) years time. **You must make the assumption that your business has been incredibly successful during this period.**

In conducting this brainstorming session be as outrageous and fanciful as you like—it is unlikely that you will get another opportunity to be so in the near future. It is important that you all feel uninhibited at this stage and do not limit yourselves either with simple extrapolations of the recent past or with restrictive 'it cannot be done' reasoning. Let your hair down, let your minds run free, imagine that you have exceeded all

YOUR VISION

♦ Record the results of your brainstorming exercise here by summarizing your vision for the next three* years:

[ ]

♦What are the key future successes that feature in your vision? List them here:

[ ]

[ ]

[ ]

[ ]

[ ]

[ ]

* You may prefer to have a one-, two-, four- or five-year vision

FIGURE 6.3

expectations by developing, introducing and selling exciting new products and services. Imagine that you have entered new markets as well as increased your share of existing ones. You may also imagine that you have streamlined your organization as well as hired and developed some of the best talent in the country.

In producing this 'first-cut' vision try to be as graphic as possible by picturing 'tangible' things that might be happening in a few years' time. Try to avoid intellectual concepts and bland generalizations. Aim to come up with exciting and interesting ideas. Furthermore make sure these ideas are expressed in 'jargon-free' terms, using down-to-earth, common sense language which everyone can understand (by picturing these ideas in their minds).

In other words, just let your imagination run wild. See yourself in the boss's seat in three years' time, congratulating your staff on having developed some wonderful new products, having conquered important new markets, having received accolades all around for your outstanding successes over the last year or two. Imagine that your business is not only financially viable in three years' time but has grown substantially during this time. Most importantly, try to think what would give you and your colleagues most satisfaction in terms of achievement.

During this initial brainstorming process it is important that you record all your visionary ideas on flip charts and exhibit them around the walls of your conference room.

VISION—THE SIX CRITICAL ATTRIBUTES

Now for the first test. Working with your team cast your eyes over all the ideas you have come up with and place a red asterisk against those which really grip your imagination, which really excite you, which—while incredibly challenging—you know instinctively can be achieved. You should remember that if you do not achieve them, someone else will— probably one of your competitors.

VISION—THE SIX CRITICAL ATTRIBUTES

◆ **Uniqueness**
 (Your vision must be different from any other)

◆ **Personal belief**
 (You must personally want to achieve this vision)

◆ **Challenging**
 (Your vision must be incredibly challenging)

◆ **Achievable**
 (Your vision must be achievable)

◆ **Simple**
 (You must be able to articulate your vision in a few paragraphs)

◆ **Graphic**
 (You must be able to explain your vision in graphic terms which everyone can relate to)

FIGURE 6.4

In other words, condense the ideas you have brainstormed into a challenging visionary picture of the future. Summarize this vision onto one chart (see Fig. 6.3).

The vision you eventually develop from this initial brainstorm will be the focal point for your business plan. As such it must be unlike any other vision the reader has come across. It must represent what you would really want to achieve for the business. Furthermore, it must be challenging as well as achievable. You have to take care to differentiate between a fantasy (which is unachievable) and a vision (which is achievable). Finally, you must be able to summarize your vision in a few paragraphs which are easy to communicate and which everyone in your organization can relate to—it must have meaning for everyone in terms of their future work. To help develop this understanding it is important that you can explain your vision in graphic terms, using vivid illustrations of how you see the future. It should be stressed that these illustrations are not prescriptive but merely an expression of how you see the vision being converted into future practice. In due course everyone in your organization should become involved in pursuing the vision and turning it into a reality for the future.

Unless you can apply these six critical attributes of your vision, it will become bland and meaningless (see Fig. 6.4 for a summary).

VALUES AND BELIEFS

Now sit back and reflect on this vision and encourage your team to answer the question:

What do we, and will we, really stand for in this business?

In other words, in projecting this picture of the future what are the fundamental values and beliefs we hold in relation to the business itself? These values and beliefs must be totally compatible with the vision you have just drawn up. Too many organizations say one thing ('these are our values') and do another, thus sending conflicting signals to both their customers and their staff. It is no good declaring in February

FUTURE THINKING—YOUR VALUES AND BELIEFS

In the light of the vision you have prepared with your team, identify the main values and beliefs upon which your business is–and will be–based

This is what we stand for in our business:

FIGURE 6.5

that you place top priority on providing a first-class service to your customers and then in November embarking on a year end cost-cutting spree which reduces service levels to them.

Figure 6.5 provides a simple form to help you articulate your values and beliefs.

Without a strong sense of vision and a cohesive set of values and beliefs you will be prone to firing off initiative after initiative in a superficial attempt to implement the latest management fashion (for example, 'quality circles' or 'total quality management'). The key is that you really believe in quality, irrespective of whether it is in fashion or not.

During the first few sessions of the three days away with your team you really need to work and rework your vision so that it becomes not only believable but has meaning for everyone in your organization. Everyone must be able to identify with it and feel they can contribute to it.

Your vision, values and beliefs must be a clear and exciting reflection of what you want to achieve for the future of the business and how you intend to get there. The more compelling your approach, the more likely you are to get support from others.

As soon as you have established a vision which you believe you can pursue in earnest, you will need to establish your strategic priority objectives.

STRATEGIC PRIORITY OBJECTIVES

Your strategic priority objectives are essentially the key targets you have to achieve over the next few years in pursuit of your vision. They form the basis for developing practical plans of implementation and thus converting the vision into a reality for the future.

The decisions you make with regard to strategic priority objectives are critical. The actions that flow out of them will have a major impact on every aspect of your business over the coming months and years. Every

EXAMPLES OF STRATEGIC PRIORITY OBJECTIVES

OUTPUT PRIORITIES

Additional output volumes from:

◆ **Strategic sales initiatives** with respect to existing products/services, existing markets, new approaches
◆ **Increasing existing production capacity**
◆ **Introduction of new product/services**
◆ **Development of new markets**

INPUT PRIORITIES

To achieve the above output priorities requires:

◆ **Increased efficiency** (production, organization, etc.)
◆ **Organization development** (recruitment, training, management development, etc.)
◆ **Product research and development** (to produce new products, etc.)
◆ **Investment in new technology** (new information systems, state-of-the-art equipment, etc.)
◆ **Investment in strategic marketing** (promotions, campaigns, market development, etc.)

FIGURE 6.6

employee will be affected by these decisions at some stage. Not only could the nature of their work change as you implement plans to introduce new products and serve new markets, but the decisions you are about to make will have a vital impact on their livelihoods and families. Inevitably your employees will interpret your vision and strategic priority objectives in terms of the impact they will have on their own jobs and future prospects.

I have come across teams of directors who have decided, as a strategic priority objective, to contract out large sections of work currently under-taken by their own people—and they have done so without due regard for the consequences. They felt it right to 'downsize' or 're-engineer' the organization.

Decisions about strategic priority objectives cannot therefore be taken in isolation. Too many organizations glibly declare, as a belief, that 'people are our most important asset' and then establish plans to kick them in the teeth by 'downsizing' (so fashionable!).

In other words, take this stage of the business planning process very seriously! In no way is business planning an academic exercise—imple-mentation of the plan will affect people's lives.

When you drive away from the hotel with your nice new vision and strategic priority objectives on a flip chart (all ready for typing up), you will have committed to a direction which has a critical impact on every-one associated with your business—your employees and their families, your suppliers, your customers and your backers.

Concentrate hard on thinking through your strategic priority objectives and how they interrelate. You and your team will need to convince yourselves that they are really achievable and that any problems experi-enced en route can be overcome. The more you convince yourselves, the more able you will be to convince others.

Some examples of 'headline' strategic priority objectives are given in Fig. 6.6 opposite. You will need to produce your own and elaborate a little more. Thus you will need to specify which markets you aim to move into, or the type of products and services you plan to develop.

FUTURE THINKING— STRATEGIC PRIORITY OBJECTIVES

Working from your vision, produce the priority strategic objectives that have to be achieved over the next year (or two) to move towards the vision.

For example, in relation to:

♦ product/service development (new products, etc.)
♦ market development (new customers, etc.)
♦ organization development (training, etc.)
♦ information and systems development
♦ financial controls (improvements to, etc.)

List these priority strategic objectives* here (use additional sheets if required):

| |
| |
| |
| |
| |
| |
| |

* In your business plan each of these priority strategic objectives will require explanation and justification

FIGURE 6.7

As you work on each strategic priority objective, remember to keep testing it against your vision, values and beliefs. Also examine carefully how each objective will impact on the others.

You will also need to think carefully about how to assess the feasibility of achieving each objective. It may well be possible to do this during your three days together. Alternatively you might need to reconvene after a few weeks having undertaken some research.

You may find Fig. 6.7 helpful in summarizing your strategic priority objectives.

Having established your vision, beliefs and strategic priority objectives for the next few years you will be ready to undertake **Step 3**, which is to quantify your objectives and convert them into financial projections.

Before you do so, and before you leave the hotel in which you have been closeted for three days, consider one final matter. What are you going to tell your people tomorrow? All your people will have been aware of the 'top team's' absence for three days. This will have generated gossip, speculation and rumours which you will need to abate with a carefully worded communiqué to be issued on your return.

You will need to assess how confidential your vision and objectives should be. Your people will have a vested interest in your decisions, and ideally you would want to communicate with them immediately and bring them into your confidence. You may even want to involve them in assessing the feasibility of your plans.

However, your competitors will also have a vested interest in knowing your future plans. So, you will need to assess the risk of your plans leaking to the competition. In fact, you are in the classic bind of wanting to be open and honest with your employees at the same time as wanting to be secretive in the face of competition.

There are two general rules which apply in these circumstances:

RIVERSIDE LEISURE—BUSINESS PLAN (Extracts)

STRATEGIC PRIORITY OBJECTIVES

The future:

◆ Riverside Leisure's aim is to increase attendances in specific areas as the result of targeted marketing. For example:
—*Junior—develop the entertainment value of the centre*
—*Family—attract young families with additional play features*
—*Health and fitness—develop the centre's market share particularly in the 'Health' area by increasing adult awareness of healthy living.*

◆ Improve overall quality of service to customers by implementing the quality audit system and developing the Customer Care and Quality Service Charter with all staff. The centre's extensive training and retraining programme for all staff will continue to help maximize customer satisfaction through staff awareness.

◆ Continued excellence in technical operation and management to maintain the quality feel to the building and finishes. Extensive knowledge of the fabric, fittings and equipment will ensure an effective implementation of planned maintenance (using highly specialized subcontractors where appropriate) to maintain high standards.

◆ Flexible staffing structure and arrangements to enable proactive responses to changes in market demands and customer requirements. Comprehensive induction systems to continue high standards of staff integration before contact with public.

◆ Continued customer based programming to maximize cross-sectional market appeal and meet the Authority's management policy demands.

◆ Customer base will continue to expand with increased participation levels as the result of heightened awareness of the benefits from regular exercise.

(Reprinted with permission)

FIGURE 6.8

◆ Never issue to your employees anything in writing (about the business as a whole) which could be taken advantage of by your competitors.

◆ Always communicate confidential information to your employees verbally and face-to-face.

The communiqué you issue, therefore, should not contain any confidential information. Should you want to take your employees into your confidence, you must do it eyeball to eyeball.

The vision and strategic priority objectives you have produced will form the basis for developing your plan. This is **Step 3** and is dealt with in the next chapter.

Figure 6.8 provides an example of the strategic priority objectives of one organization, Riverside Leisure.

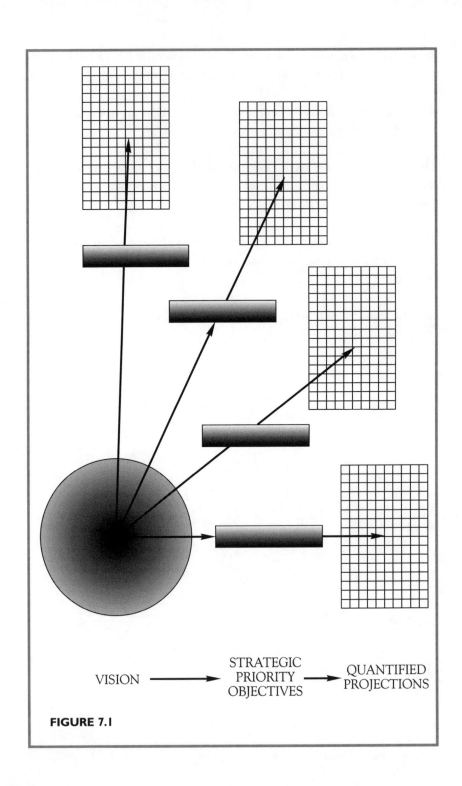

VISION ⟶ STRATEGIC PRIORITY OBJECTIVES ⟶ QUANTIFIED PROJECTIONS

FIGURE 7.1

THE SUCCESSFUL MANAGER'S GUIDE TO BUSINESS PLANNING

STEP 3—DEVELOPING YOUR PLAN

7

> ❝*You read a book from the beginning to the end. You run a business the opposite way. You start with the end, and then you do everything you must to reach it.*❞
>
> Harold Geneen, CEO IT&T, *Managing* 1984

You now need to develop a plan which includes a series of quantified targets which derive from the strategic priority objectives. The financial implications of achieving these targets are a critical consideration and will need to be spelt out clearly.

So far, all you have is a set of words describing your vision and your strategic priority objectives. To achieve any credibility and meaning these fine words now have to be converted into real quantified targets and financial projections. In other words, you will need to draw from your strategic priority objectives a clear set of output and input projections which will yield a bottom line figure acceptable to those whose approval you are seeking.

If you are working for a commercial company and have profit centre accountability this bottom line will, in fact, be your profit level. If you are working for a non-commercial public sector organization, this bottom line may well be a balanced budget.

Whatever organization you work for, there is no way you will be able to proceed with your plan if your projections demonstrate a long-term loss as a result of achieving your vision. (Your 'funders' may well tolerate a loss in the initial stage, although you will have to justify this.)

OUTPUT PROJECTION

Vision:
To develop our business from being a 'small-scale' supplier of type XYZ products in the local market-place to become a leading regional supplier.

Strategic priority objective '1'

◆ To increase unit sales of 'Product X' in Areas A, B and C by 5% per annum.

◆ To mount a campaign to market and sell 'Product X' in Area D.

Quantified projection (extract)

	UNIT SALES—PRODUCT 'X'			
	This year	Year 1	Year 2	Year 3
Areas A, B, C	1000	1050	1103	1158
Area D	0	100	160	220
Total sales				
Product 'X'	1000	1150	1263	1378
Price*	£100	£104	£108	£112
Total Revenue	£100 000	£119 600	£136 404	£154 336

*Pricing assumptions
1. All figures assume zero inflation
2. Product 'X' will be enhanced with additional low cost features warranting a price increase, in real terms of 4% per annum

FIGURE 7.2

QUANTIFYING OUTPUTS

In producing the projections you will need to quantify existing output levels (defined through **Step 3**) and then quantify how these will change as a result of moving towards your strategic priority objectives.

The process is not as complex as it may seem. All you will need to do is some simple mathematics—or perhaps avail yourself of a simple spreadsheet model on your computer to assess the impact of different assumptions on your output and input levels.

Figure 7.2 gives a simplified example of an output projection. First of all you will need to project the increase in sales for each different type of account (in this case 'Product X'). You will then need to make certain assumptions about how you will price 'Product X' over the next three years. From these, you will be able to project the revenue generated from achieving this strategic priority objective.

The same process (**Vision** → **Strategic objectives** → **Quantitative assumptions** → **Projections**) can equally be applied for each different type of output.

In attempting this first pass at projecting outputs and inputs it is wise to be conservative. In other words, you should present the **worst possible case**:

> Assume:

> ◆ Lowest possible revenue from outputs

> ◆ Highest costs for all your inputs

Figure 7.10 and 7.11 at the end of this chapter, provide an example of how Riverside Leisure project their outputs.

It is relatively easy to construct a simple spreadsheet on your computer to examine the impact on your output projections of various assumptions relating to price and production levels. Even if you don't have a computer

QUANTIFY YOUR VISIONARY PLANS

Convert your priority strategic objectives into outputs, inputs and money

Summary projections– (annual)	Measure (units)	Year 1 No. of units	Year 2 No. of units	Year 3 No. of units	Revenue–income Year 1 £	Year 2 £	Year 3 £
OUTPUTS							
(units 'sold' and revenue income)							
TOTAL OUTPUTS							
INPUTS						COSTS	
(units 'bought' and unit costs)							
TOTAL INPUTS							

FIGURE 7.3

the manual calculations should not prove too difficult. A simple template for this purpose is provided on the page opposite (see Fig. 7.3).

You will need to project revenue for each product (or service) category. You should clearly spell out in your business plan the assumptions you make in every case. For example, if you are a professional service company you will need to specify your assumptions with regard to the percentage chargeable time for each category of staff. Or if you are a training company selling distant learning packages, you will need to state the assumptions you make regarding price as well as the number of potential purchasers of each type of package.

You should go through the same output projection process even if you are a manager of an internal business unit in an organization where no internal trading takes place. In this case it is wise to establish a 'notional price' in order to establish 'notional reveue'. This will enable you to compare your 'business unit' with those of your competitors, especially in terms of price. It will also enable you to respond positively if there is a sudden requirement to put you on to a real business footing (i.e. internal or external trading).

NOTIONAL FIGURES

By using 'notional' figures you will be able to establish whether your internal business unit is potentially viable or not. Viability can only be established by deducting the cost of inputs from the revenue generated by output.

Figure 7.4 on the next page gives an example of how a training section in personnel services uses notional figures in a business plan.

Developing your plan will prove quite time consuming. Using the template shown, or a variation of it, you can project the impact on output levels of achieving each of your strategic priority objectives.

PERSONNEL SERVICES TRAINING SECTION— BUSINESS PLAN

Notional figures are your best estimates of income and costs. In this example, notional figures are in italics.

Management training

20 × two-day appraisal courses @ £3000 per course (confirmed)	60 000	
15 × one-day supervisors' workshops @ £1500 per workshop	*22 500*	
5 × five-day leadership seminars @ £8000 per seminar	*40 000*	
10 × two-day team-building workshops @ £3000 per workshop	*30 000*	£152 500

General training (all confirmed)

30 × one-day customer workshops @ £1200 per workshop	36 000	
10 × half-day health and safety refresher courses @ £500	5000	
20 × one-day equal opportunities workshops @ £1200	24 000	£65 000

Consultancy (all confirmed)

Development of training strategy for operations 10 days consultancy @ £500	5000	
Needs analysis for sales and marketing—agreed fee	4000	
Consultancy advice to sister company 10 days @ £500	5000	£14 000
REVENUE TOTAL		**£231 500**

Consultants' fees

Hire of external consultants and trainers	*30 000*	£30 000

Conference accommodation

Hire of hotels facilities	*20 000*	
Printing of leaflets (committed)	4000	
Production of training manuals (committed)	20 000	£44 000

Staff costs

Basic staff costs including expenses (committed)	120 000	£120 000

Others

Purchase of new training equipment	*10 000*	
Central charges	*27 500*	£37 500
COSTS TOTAL		**£231 500**

FIGURE 7.4

QUANTIFYING INPUTS

The same process should be repeated to project your 'inputs'. Again you will need to examine the impact of achieving each of your strategic priority objectives on your inputs. The same template (Fig. 7.3) can be used. On the next page (Fig. 7.5) is a list of common examples of 'inputs' which you may use as a checklist.

It is normal to differentiate between fixed costs and variable (direct) costs. Fixed costs are overheads such as salaries, rent, and related charges and do not vary directly in relation to output volumes. Variable costs, such as those of raw materials, vary directly in relation to output volumes. Your financial adviser will be able to advise you on this as well as on items relating to capital expenditure and depreciation. For the purpose of developing your input projection, it is advisable to show all projected costs, including capital expenditure. These can be separated at the next stage into your balance sheet, profit and loss account and cash flow projections.

STATING ASSUMPTIONS

As with your outputs, it is important that you clearly state your assumptions when projecting your inputs. Any substantial changes over existing levels will need to be highlighted. For example if you project a need to hire more staff, or lease a new computer, or spend a substantial sum on advertising and printing, then this must be highlighted in your plan.

To preserve the 'uniqueness' of your business and achieve your vision some investment will, inevitably, be required. Your business plan will not be credible unless these investments are clearly shown and justified. In developing your plan you should be able to demonstrate how the investment input can be converted into tangible output revenue. Thus there would be no point in investing in a major training and development programme for all your people unless you can demonstrate how this would bear fruit in terms of increased revenue output generation towards achieving your vision.

INPUT CATEGORIES—AN EXAMPLE CHECKLIST

Direct costs
◆ Cost of raw materials and other supplies
◆ Delivery costs

Overheads
◆ Staff costs (Salaries, bonuses, National Insurance contributions, pensions, health care, etc.)
◆ Training courses
◆ Recruitment costs
◆ Travel and subsistence
◆ Motor expenses
◆ Rent and related charges (electricity, service charges, etc.)
◆ Professional services (accountancy, legal, etc.)
◆ Sales promotion expenses and advertising
◆ Printing
◆ Stationery and related supplies
◆ Telephones
◆ Repairs and renewals
◆ Insurance (buildings, contents, equipment, etc.)
◆ Computer leasing and software
◆ Bank charges and interest
◆ Entertainment

FIGURE 7.5

Expressed another way, your case for any investment—whether it be in computers, plant or people—must be well argued in terms of achieving your strategic priority objectives and vision. That argument must be demonstrated in a quantified way through your output and input projections.

Having projected both outputs and inputs and converted them into crude financial figures you will be able to establish an initial bottom line figure.

Commercial organization	*Public sector organization*
Revenue from outputs less (−) **Cost of inputs = Profit**	**Revenue from outputs =** **Costs of inputs** (Ideal balance)

In a public sector organization the revenue from outputs should, ideally, equal the cost of inputs, whereas in a commercial organization the difference—if positive—is the 'added value' which is the source of potential profit.

With the establishment of internal trading, more and more public sector organizations are effectively generating notional revenue figures relating to outputs. As stressed before, this helps to avoid the danger of a sole focus on inputs and costs. By relating output revenue to input costs you will be able to establish measures of 'value for money' and prevent costs getting out of control—the traditional problem of large public sector organizations.

UNIT COSTS

The basis for 'value for money' measures are 'unit costs' which can be defined as follows:

$$\text{Unit cost} = \frac{\text{Revenue from selling one unit of output}}{\text{Cost of producing one output unit}}$$

Knowing your unit costs is critical for any business manager.

CASH FLOW

	Produce a monthly analysis to support each of the financial figures												
Detailed analysis (£)	Year ☐ Month by month analysis (£)												
	1	2	3	4	5	6	7	8	9	10	11	12	Year total
OUTPUTS													
(cash flow in from sales)													
TOTAL OUTPUTS A													
INPUTS													
(cash flow out from expenditure)													
TOTAL INPUTS B													
CASH BALANCE A–B													
OPENING BALANCE													
CLOSING BALANCE													

FIGURE 7.6

Having developed your plan into a crude set of output and input projections, you will now need to seek the help of your financial adviser to help you convert these figures into a set of projected financial figures, presented in a form which accountants, bankers and other financial experts like to see them. In other words you will need to develop the following:

◆ **Cash flow projections**

◆ **Balance sheet projections**

◆ **Profit and loss projections**

If you are already trained in accountancy or finance you will find this easy. Even if you aren't, it is worth having a stab at these projections before you seek the help of your financial adviser.

CASH FLOW PROJECTIONS

To produce these, take the first year of your output and input projections and produce a detailed month by month analysis. This will enable you to demonstrate seasonal variations and plan your expenditure accordingly. From this it is a simple matter to produce a cash flow projection (see Fig. 7.6).

In the commercial world, cash flow is vital and—in the short term—more important than profitability. Unless you have enough cash to pay your bills you will go bankrupt, it is as simple as that. Your cash flow projections must demonstrate that you have enough cash coming in to keep you operational. In developing your projections you will therefore need to consider how quickly your customers (debtors) will pay you and how these payments balance with your regular and irregular items of expenditure on inputs such as salaries, rent and consumables as well as, of course, tax and VAT.

ASSETS/LIABILITIES

	Itemize planned changes to your assets and liabilities			
ASSETS	Description (highlight changes/ investments, etc.)	Year 1 £	Year 2 £	Year 3 £
(suggested headings)				
TANGIBLE FIXED ASSETS				
DEBTORS				
LIABILITIES				
CREDITORS				

(Note: This is your initial list. You will need help from your financial adviser to complete it)

FIGURE 7.7

CAPITAL REQUIREMENTS

In parallel with developing your cash flow projections, you will need to project your capital requirements in terms of planned changes to your assets and liabilities.

This will not only form a basis for the projected balance sheets in your plan but will also enable you to refine your cash flow projections. Figure 7.7 opposite provides a simple template to itemize the key changes that you intend to make in achieving your strategic priority objectives.

Thus under changes to assets could come:

◆ Investment in a new computer system

◆ Purchase of a new company car

◆ Purchase of furniture and equipment

◆ Projected increases or decreases of money owed to you by customers.

Under changes to liabilities could come:

◆ Additional loans from banks

◆ Projected increases or decreases of money owed by you to suppliers

◆ Increases to share capital

If you are a manager of an internal business unit, whether in the private or public sector, you may be worried about having to establish tangible assets and liabilities for your business plan, given that your organization as a corporate entity tends to own all the assets and manage centrally the liabilities. As a result you may view this part of the business planning process as fruitless and rather academic.

It should not be. It is important that you make an attempt to measure and plan for these assets and liabilities. One of the key points in this book

PROFIT PROJECTION

REVENUE	Summarize the profits you plan to make over the next 3 years					
	Two years ago	One year ago	This year	Year 1	Year 2	Year 3
TOTAL REVENUE						
COSTS						
TOTAL COSTS						
PROFIT						

FIGURE 7.8

THE SUCCESSFUL MANAGER'S GUIDE TO BUSINESS PLANNING

is that to differentiate a 'business plan' from an 'ordinary' management plan you have to 'think business'. Thinking business means a critical consideration of your assets and liabilities—past, present and future. If you cannot do this, in no way are you entitled to describe your plan as a 'business plan'.

As an internal manager of a business unit you must, therefore, be prepared to estimate your assets and liabilities using notional figures if necessary. By doing so you may discover some amazing things about your business. First, you could discover that what you thought of as assets are not in fact assets but merely input costs. For example, say you plan to acquire a new computer system which will be procured on your behalf by Corporate IT. Who owns the asset? Unless Corporate IT assigns ownership of the new computer system to you, in no way can you show it on the balance sheet for your business unit. You must, therefore, consider it to be 'rented' or 'leased' from Corporate IT, with charges which will show through on your input projections. The charges can be identified through internal trading accounts where used.

The same applies to other items such as property and equipment.

In other words, as an internal business manager your assets and liabilities may be minimal—most items of capital expenditure showing through as 'rental' or 'lease' costs on the profit and loss account. However, you must be prepared to answer the question: 'How would all this change if my business unit suddenly became a stand-alone business?' (that is, a limited company of which you are chief executive).

PROFIT PROJECTIONS

The final step in developing your plan is to project your profit levels. This is perhaps the most exciting part of the process. This will be your first attempt at establishing a 'bottom line' and at proving whether the pursuit of your vision and achievement of your strategic priority objectives is a viable proposition.

BCC MARKETING SERVICES LTD—BUSINESS PLAN

	April	May	June	July	Aug.	Sept.	Oct.	Nov.	Dec.	Jan.	Feb.	March
Sales												
Day shift	19 398	18 494	20 982	22 795	18 285	24 341	27 387	24 642	18 391	22 823	20 797	24 400
Evening shifts	6396	6144	5439	5545	?857	4400	6240	6716	3945	2639	4400	6200
TOTAL	25 794	24 638	26 421	28 340	21 142	28 741	33 627	31 358	22 336	25 462	25 197	30 600
Cost of Sales												
Wages -D.	3862	3683	4176	4535	3641	4845	5451	4903	3662	4552	4138	4857
Wages -E.	1584	1521	1346	1374	709	1089	1544	1663	978	653	1089	1529
Line Charges -D.	2051	1956	2218	2409	1934	2573	2895	2604	1945	2413	2198	2586
Line Charges -E.	560	538	476	486	251	385	546	588	346	231	385	543
Subcontracted	1445	1156	1156	1445		1156	1445	1156			1156	1156
TOTAL	9502	8854	9372	10 249	6535	10 048	11 881	10 914	6931	7849	8966	10 671
Gross margin	16 292	15 784	17 049	18 091	14 607	18 693	21 746	20 444	15 405	17 613	16 231	19 929
Overheads												
Salaries	5271	5271	5271	5271	5271	5271	5271	5271	5271	5271	5271	5271
Secretarial	1107	885	1325	1018	770	770	963	770	770	963	770	770
Rent	758	758	758	758	758	758	758	758	758	758	758	758
Rates		165	165	165	165	165	165	165	165	165	165	165
Services Charges	221	221	221	221	221	221	221	221	221	221	221	221
Insurance	744	744	744	744	744	744	744	744	744	744	744	744
Admin phones	394	394	394	394	394	394	394	394	394	394	394	394
Equip. hire	1524	1524	1524	1524	1524	1524	1724	1724	1724	1724	1724	1724
Motor expenses	982	982	982	982	982	982	982	982	982	982	982	982
Staff admin./training	150	150	150	150	150	150	150	150	150	150	150	150
Post	200	200	200	200	200	200	200	200	200	200	200	200
Cleaning	95	95	95	95	95	95	95	95	95	95	95	95
Maintenance	200	200	200	200	200	200	200	200	200	200	200	200
Sundries	320	320	320	320	320	320	320	320	320	320	320	320
Print	167	167	167	167	167	167	167	167	167	167	167	167
Promotion	600	600	600	600	600	600	600	600	600	600	600	600
Contingencies	300	300	300	300	300	300	300	300	300	300	300	300
Professional exp.	500	500	500	500	500	500	500	500	500	500	500	500
TOTAL	13 533	13 476	13 916	13 609	13 361	13 361	13 754	13 561	13 561	13 754	13 561	13 396
Financial charges and depreciation	1500	1500	1500	1500	1500	1500	1275	1275	1275	1275	1275	1275
Total expenditure	24 535	23 830	24 788	25 358	21 396	24 909	26 910	25 750	21 767	22 878	23 802	25 342
Profit/loss	1259	808	1633	2982	− 254	3832	6717	5608	569	2584	1395	5258
Cumulative profit	1259	2067	3700	6682	6428	10 260	16 977	22 585	23 154	25 738	27 133	32 391

(D. = day
E. = evening)

(Reprinted with permission)

FIGURE 7.9

Figure 7.8 provides a simple template for this. All you need to do is extract the summary (output) revenue figures and the summary (input) cost figures you previously developed (Fig. 7.3) and subtract the latter from the former. If the answer is positive, you are in profit!

If the answer is negative do not worry! You have not even written your plan at this stage. You will need to have a second pass (iteration) at developing your plan, perhaps reviewing your pricing strategy, or your ideas about investing in the business, or your output projections (have you been too conservative?).

In developing your plan you will need to walk a tightrope between refining your figures to achieve profitability and undermining their cred-ibility by using outrageous assumptions. Whatever refinements you end up with to achieve profitability, you have to believe that these figures are really achievable. If you do not believe the figures, no one else will.

If you are a business manager in the public sector you might consider it inappropriate to work towards a profit and prefer to show a balance between revenue and costs. This may be unwise. Even money has a cost! Ideally, your output revenue should exceed your input costs by some small percentage to cover a notional interest you would have incurred if you had borrowed the money to pay for the work done (cost of inputs) in delivering the output to your customer. In simple terms, there will be a time lapse between spending (say) £100 000 on inputs and generating an output revenue of £100 000 as a result of these inputs. That gap represents a real cost in terms of the cost of money (interest charges) and should appear in your projections. The sensible practice, if you are in the public sector, is to allow a small surplus (profit) to cover these costs. Your financial adviser will indicate the conventions as far as your organization is concerned.

USING FINANCIAL ADVISERS

It is very important that you seek the help of your financial adviser to convert your crude projections into credible financial figures. No matter how good you are as a business manager in projecting cash flow, balance

RIVERSIDE LEISURE—OUTPUT CATEGORY 1: POOL

Building up a projection of outputs and converting into revenue

Sub-category 1A Swims by type	Unit of output		
Detailed output type	Tickets	Price	Revenue projected
Family peak non-members	11 250	8.00	90 000
Adult peak non-members	55 000	3.20	176 000
Junior peak non-members	70 000	1.65	115 500
Spectator peak non-members	11 000	0.75	8250
Adult off peak non-members	18 000	1.75	31 500
Junior off peak non-members	12 000	1.45	17 400
Parents/toddlers off peak n/m	16 500	1.75	28 875
60+ non-members	8000	1.25	10 000
Disabled non-members	2000	1.25	2500
Spectators off peak n/m	3500	0.60	2100
Daybreakers	8000	1.60	12 800
Family peak members	4000	5.30	21 200
Adult peak members	7000	2.20	15 400
Junior peak members	5000	1.20	6000
Adult off peak members	2000	1.45	2900
Junior off peak members	1000	1.20	100
Parents/toddlers o/p mem	1300	1.45	1885
60+ members	3600	1.00	3600
Disabled members	300	1.00	300
Family special	100	11.50	1150
Adult special	100	3.75	375
Junior special	0	3.75	0
Leisure pool		Total	**548 935**

Sub-category 1B Wet side activities			
Detailed output type			
Parent/baby	1728	2.70	4666
Parent/toddler	2074	2.70	599
Starfish	480	4.20	216
Penguins	1920	4.20	8064
Seals	1920	4.20	8064
Dolphins	1382	4.20	5806
Sharks	1037	4.20	4355
Challenge	525	4.70	2467
Crash courses	263	2.40	630
Ante-/post-natal	1728	2.40	4147
Adult	1166	2.70	3149
Life saving	256	5.20	1331
50+	918	1.20	1101
School lessons	1538	1.40	2150
Aqua fit	4914	3.70	18 182
Wet side		Total	**71 727**
Sub-category 1C other activities		Total	**38 979**
GRAND TOTAL			659 641
less VAT @ 17.5%			−98 244
NET TOTAL			561 397

Profit/loss account Revenue Year 1

Pool	561 397
Fitness suite	185 596
Catering	205 000
Bar	40 000
Moorings	10 000
Mini golf	2500
Car park	59 000
Sponsorship	2500
TOTAL	1 065 993
(See Fig. 7.11)	

FIGURE 7.10

Adapted from the Business Plan produced by Riverside Leisure (reprinted with permission)

sheets and profits, you will not be in a position to take account of all the financial conventions, financial regulations and laws unless you are a fully trained accountant. Financial probity and compliance are essential for the integrity of your plan and to instil confidence in your readers.

TESTING THE PLAN

Having developed your plan, you are ready to put it to the test. You will need to gather up all the facts, figures and projections, together with your vision and strategic objectives, to convert them into some crude documentary form which is intelligible to other people. This is your 'first-cut' plan. No semblance of the finished version is required at this stage. However, if other people are to understand it, a logical and coherent presentation of how you have developed your plan and arrived at your decisions will be needed.

Figure 7.9 gives an example of an extract of the business plan of BCC Marketing Services Ltd and shows the output projections (sales) and input projections (costs and overheads) for one year.

RIVERSIDE LEISURE— BUSINESS PLAN EXTRACT

PROJECTION OF REVENUE FROM OUTPUTS (income)

Summary sheet

Income	Year 1	Year 2	Year 3	Year 4	Year 5
Leisure pool	561 397	547 363	585 678	597 391	567 522
Fitness suite	185 596	193 020	202 671	210 777	202 346
Catering	205 000	199 875	213 866	213 866	198 896
Bar	40 000	39 000	42 510	44 636	41 065
Moorings	10 000	10 500	11 025	11 025	11 025
Mini golf	2500	2625	2625	2625	2625
Car park	59 000	57 525	60 401	60 401	60 401
Sponsorship	2500	3750	5250	5775	6064
TOTAL INCOME	1 065 993	1 053 657	1 124 026	1 146 497	1 089 943

(Reprinted with permission)

FIGURE 7.11

RATE YOUR PLAN AGAINST THE SEVEN KEYS

	Comments	Rating*
♦ Thinking business		
♦ Uniqueness		
♦ Vision and belief		
♦ Outputs and inputs		
♦ Credibility and risk		
♦ Targeted style		
♦ Indestructibility		

*1 = poor
5 = excellent

Undertake this rating as soon as you have completed the first-cut of your plan and again when you have produced the final version

FIGURE 8.1

STEP 4—CHALLENGING YOUR PLAN

> ❝*This morning my Lord showed me the King's declaration and his letter to the two Generals to be communicated to the fleet. Upon receipt of it my Lord summoned a council of war (the first that hath been in my time). Which done, the commanders all came on board where I read the letter and declaration. Not one man seemed to say no to it, though I am confident many in their hearts were against it.*❞
>
> From the *Diary of Samuel Pepys*, 3rd May 1660

All the good work you have done so far in developing your first-cut business plan from your vision and strategic priority objectives now needs to be challenged. This means applying some critical tests to this first-cut plan.

Before you even consider this, however, there is one vital thing you must do—you must 'sleep on your plan'. In practice this means locking your first-cut plan away in a drawer and forgetting about it for a week. Do not let anyone dissuade you from doing this—whatever the pressures may be. If you attempt to test your plan immediately after writing it you will fail, mainly because you will see the plan in the same light as when you wrote it.

A DIFFERENT LIGHT

To challenge your plan in an effective way, it is vital that you see it in a different light. So allow yourself to be distracted by other matters, or go on holiday for a week. If you really cannot let go, challenge someone else's business plan.

CHALLENGING THE PLAN

A test strategy:
- ◆ First test run—self-driven
- ◆ Second test run—your team
- ◆ Third test run—a third party
  (The nastiest accountant around)
- ◆ Fourth test run—your boss

Test criteria:
- ◆ The common sense test
- ◆ The fact and figure test
- ◆ The credibility test (testing of assumptions)
- ◆ The sensitivity test (worst case <> best case)
- ◆ The test of critical ratios
- ◆ The attitude test

FIGURE 8.2

A TEST STRATEGY

After sleeping on the plan for at least a week, spend a little time preparing for the challenge. This means developing a test strategy (Fig. 8.2).

While you will find it time-consuming you will certainly find it worth while if you put your first-cut plan through four different test runs:

◆ First test run—self-driven

◆ Second test run—your team

◆ Third test run—a third party (the nastiest accountant around)

◆ Fourth test run—your boss

FIRST TEST RUN—SELF-DRIVEN

While the first test run will be conducted by you, you will have to forget yourself to make it effective! It is important that you put yourself in the shoes of one of your key readers (see Fig. 4.2). For example, if your plan is primarily aimed at your bank manager, then try to imagine you are that bank manager and try to react how he or she might respond on studying your plan. Try to think through what tests he or she would apply to your plan—and then apply these tests to the plan. For example, there are certain key ratios which should apply (see Fig. 8.7). As an initial test you should also rate your plan against the 'seven keys' for a successful business plan (see Fig. 8.1).

SECOND TEST RUN—YOUR TEAM

Having put your plan through your own self-driven mill, it is wise to present the plan to your team and ask them to give it a thorough going over. This is where you have to be very brave. The danger is that you take any criticism they make personally, that you get defensive, that you accuse them of not understanding, or of being difficult. The fear is that you may dismiss their constructive ideas and fail to listen to their positive suggestions. No matter how closely you have worked with your

TEST RESULTS

Test no:		
Criteria	Comments	Date

FIGURE 8.3

THE SUCCESSFUL MANAGER'S GUIDE TO BUSINESS PLANNING

team in developing the plan, ultimately it will be your 'personal baby' and you will feel (and be) directly accountable for it.

If teamwork has any meaning at all it is to challenge the boss in a helpful way. You are the boss—perhaps to be challenged by your team. In fact you must encourage them to tear your (and their) plan apart and put it back together again. It is critical that you believe in the plan, and that they do too. Too many teams pay lip service to their boss's plans and rubbish them behind his or her back. The last thing you want to happen is for your team to say 'I told you so' when your plan is in danger of rejection from the very people whose approval you need. And it will be rejected if you do not have the support of your team.

The more criticism your plan receives from your team, the stronger it will become. The criticism you invite will not relate to your vision and strategic priority objectives (your team have already committed themselves to these) but to the facts, figures, assumptions and projections that you have developed during **Step 3**.

THIRD TEST RUN—A THIRD PARTY

As soon as you have passed the 'team test' it is worth inviting a third party to have a crack at pulling it apart and finding fault. One area in which you could still be vulnerable is on the financial side.

Hopefully you will have engaged a financial adviser during **Step 3** to help you develop the financial figures. If so, find another one who can offer an independent view of the figures produced. Ideally you should find the nastiest accountant around, who can expose the holes in your plan. Nasty accountants are those who excel at assessing the financial logic of your arguments and who are quick to spot the fundamental flaw which everyone else has missed. Such accountants really are a pain in the neck—but they do provide an invaluable service to managers who are financially short-sighted.

Depending on the nature of your business, you might well want to use other third parties to test out your plan. Inevitably, most of these third parties will charge an expensive fee for the pleasure of picking holes in

PREPARE TO MEET YOUR BOSS

Before you present your first-cut plan to your boss, try to anticipate the type of question he or she will ask you and prepare some answers.

Anticipated questions:

1	
2	
3	
4	
5	
6	

Your prepared answers:

1	
2	
3	
4	
5	
6	

FIGURE 8.4

your hard work, but it really is a worthwhile investment. Your plan could easily sink without trace at the approval stage if it has not been subjected to the severest scrutiny by the best expertise you can lay your hands on.

FOURTH TEST RUN—YOUR BOSS

The fourth and final test ideally should be a formality. This involves testing the plan on your boss. In the perfect world you will have an excellent relationship with your boss and will have involved him or her in the early stages of establishing your vision and strategic priority objectives. If your boss is an autocrat it could well be that he or she has imposed some such objectives upon you—on behalf of the organization as a whole. In other words, your boss may well have charged you with achieving critical organization goals and demanded a business plan from you in relation to these.

Whatever the style of your boss, it is highly probable that he or she will not have been involved in the 'nitty-gritty' **Step 3** process of developing your plan. It is, therefore, important to invite him or her to put your plan to the test by challenging every aspect of it. This is not the same as seeking approval. It could well be that he or she is the 'key reader' whom the plan is aimed at, and it is his or her approval you are eventually seeking. You should therefore make it clear to your boss that you are **not** seeking approval at this stage, but just testing out the plan.

In practice, relationships with bosses will vary enormously and there is no one prescription on how to handle this stage of the business planning process. You will have to make your own judgement as when best to involve your boss in establishing your vision and strategic priority objectives and in challenging your plan. Whatever the subsequent course of events, you will not be able to proceed without his or her formal approval.

TEST CRITERIA

The four test runs can be conducted using some simple criteria. These are:

OVERALL TEST RESULTS

Criteria	Comments	Date
Common sense test		
The fact and figure test		
The credibility test		
The sensitivity test		
The test of critical ratios		
The attitude test		

FIGURE 8.5

◆ The common sense test

◆ The fact and figure test

◆ The credibility test (testing of assumptions)

◆ The sensitivity test (worst case <> best case)

◆ The test of critical ratios

◆ The attitude test

THE COMMON SENSE TEST

The common sense test is a simple 'read through' test to identify anything in your first-cut plan which jars or which obviously does not make sense. It is important to be fresh and open-minded when you undertake this read through test. Remember that you have been so immersed in developing your plan over recent weeks that you may have blindly missed an obvious error of judgement that could subsequently undermine everything. Therefore, be prepared for shocks—all may not now appear as it first seemed. In addition to obvious errors of judgement, there could be obvious errors of omission. Thus you could have failed to take into account a critical factor in projecting your output revenues (for example, that one of your competitors is moving in on your market).

THE FACT AND FIGURE TEST

The second test criteria relates to all your facts and figures. Quite simply, they must **all** be correct—every single one of them. Honesty is vital here. Never pass off a 'guestimate' as a fact. If you are guessing, assuming, or using notional figures, be honest and say so. Check your facts, go back to the original data and double check. Ensure that every fact and figure can be substantiated under challenge. The same applies to any deductions you make. If you say 'The average cost of printing each leaflet run over the last year has been £1000' you will need to demonstrate (on being challenged) how you arrived at that average. Another example would be if you state that your competitors charge £500 for this product. Your

KEY RATIOS

List the key ratios by which you believe your business will be judged. Some examples of key ratios are provided in Fig. 8.7 over the page.

Key ratios for your business unit

1	
2	
3	
4	
5	
6	
7	
8	
9	
10	
E.g. no. of output units p.a.	*Per employee*

FIGURE 8.6

readers might well check up on this fact, so be prepared to demonstrate—with tariff sheets if necessary—that this £500 figure is accurate.

THE CREDIBILITY TEST

Your business plan will inevitably be based on a set of assumptions used for projecting the future. These assumptions need to be tested for credibility. For example, an assumption that the demand for your type of product will increase by 50 per cent in three years would normally not be credible—unless you can substantiate this assumption with a convincing argument. Blind faith and outrageous optimism are insufficient to sustain a business plan. Justification is required at every step. Action plans based on unsound assumptions can prove disastrous and will inevitably be exposed by your readers. Ultimately, there is an issue of judgement involved in backing your assumptions about the future and the risks involved. In analysing your assumptions you will need to assess the risk. For example an assumption that your customers would bear a price increase of five per cent when you upgrade your product with additional features is, in the end, a risk judgement that you and your approvers have to make.

THE SENSITIVITY TEST

The risks, to a certain extent, can be evaluated using this next test which is based on a sensitivity analysis. During **Step 3** you were advised to assume the worst possible case in projecting the future. This means assuming the lowest possible output revenue and the highest possible costs for your inputs.

The figures you use in your plan should be tested by examining the impact of a series of variations on your figures. For example, what would be the impact on your bottom line profit figure if your competitors moved in with a price-cutting attack and you were unable to sustain a planned five per cent price increase? Conversely, what would be the impact if exchange rates moved in your favour and you were able to purchase supplies of foreign components at five per cent less than you had planned?

KEY RATIOS—EXAMPLES

◆ Profit/sales

◆ Profit/costs

◆ Profit/employees

◆ Profit/value of assets

◆ Sales/value of inventory

◆ Overheads/total costs

◆ Sales/total costs

◆ Debtors/sales

◆ Creditors/sales

◆ Value of order book/annual sales

◆ Percentage turnover of employees

◆ Cost of training/total costs

◆ Cost of marketing/total costs

◆ Output units/employees

◆ Number of 'direct' employees/total employees

◆ Unit costs

FIGURE 8.7

In other words, even with all your expertise, you will be unable to predict the future with 100 per cent accuracy. Therefore, you need to estimate the impact of variations of up to, say, ± 10 per cent on your key figures and indicate how sensitive your bottom line is to these variations. This sensitivity analysis will provide some measure of the risks involved and the degree of uncertainty inherent in your plan.

THE TEST OF CRITICAL RATIOS

This test is based on key ratios. Any investor seeking to put funds into a company will always examine certain key ratios as a measure of success. These can be simple, added value ratios such as profit/sales and profit/costs. Other ratios may include sales/employees or sales/value of inventory. Each of these key ratios will, of course, have to be adapted depending on the nature of the business. For example there are many industry-specific ratios such as 'percentage room occupancy' or 'percentage revenue from food and beverages/total revenue' in the hotel business. In the professional services business 'percentage chargeable time' is a key ratio. In any business the ratio of 'overheads/total costs' is an important test of potential viability.

You will need to decide what the key ratios are in your line of business and establish the norms against which your plan can be tested. These norms can be developed by historical analysis and by comparison with your competitors. While your plan will need to demonstrate long-term improvements in certain key ratios, wild variations will invoke suspicion in your readers and will need to be checked out and justified. For example, nobody is going to believe you if the ratios indicate that 'profit per employee' is going to double within a year—unless a central part of your plan is to contract out much of the work currently undertaken by your people.

Liaise with your team and your advisers to draw up a list of key ratios against which the projections in your plan can be tested. Figure 8.7 provides some examples of key ratios which are frequently used. You will need to adapt them to the specific type of business you are in. The list is, of course, not exhaustive.

Take care not to 'invent' too many key ratios. Put yourself in the shoes of your key readers and try to think of the key ratios against which they will test your plan.

THE ATTITUDE TEST

The final test is one of 'attitude'. Plans will never be accepted and approved unless a positive attitude shows through. This means a plan which demonstrates confidence but not over-optimism, which demonstrates a serious and professional approach as opposed to a sloppy 'can't be bothered to get the facts right' style. Your plan must be a fair reflection of your own thoughts, beliefs and personality as opposed to a mechanistic concoction put together using a soulless form-filling process. Having applied all the other tests, study your plan again and assess how positive and confident it seems. This will be reinforced to a high degree when you have involved your team, your boss and your closest advisers in the process.

WRITING YOUR PLAN— TEMPLATE

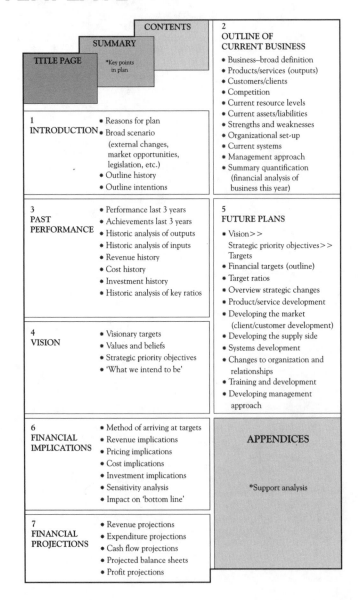

TITLE PAGE

SUMMARY
*Key points in plan

CONTENTS

2
OUTLINE OF CURRENT BUSINESS
- Business–broad definition
- Products/services (outputs)
- Customers/clients
- Competition
- Current resource levels
- Current assets/liabilities
- Strengths and weaknesses
- Organizational set-up
- Current systems
- Management approach
- Summary quantification (financial analysis of business this year)

1
INTRODUCTION
- Reasons for plan
- Broad scenario (external changes, market opportunities, legislation, etc.)
- Outline history
- Outline intentions

3
PAST PERFORMANCE
- Performance last 3 years
- Achievements last 3 years
- Historic analysis of outputs
- Historic analysis of inputs
- Revenue history
- Cost history
- Investment history
- Historic analysis of key ratios

5
FUTURE PLANS
- Vision>>
  Strategic priority objectives>>
  Targets
- Financial targets (outline)
- Target ratios
- Overview strategic changes
- Product/service development
- Developing the market (client/customer development)
- Developing the supply side
- Systems development
- Changes to organization and relationships
- Training and development
- Developing management approach

4
VISION
- Visionary targets
- Values and beliefs
- Strategic priority objectives
- 'What we intend to be'

6
FINANCIAL IMPLICATIONS
- Method of arriving at targets
- Revenue implications
- Pricing implications
- Cost implications
- Investment implications
- Sensitivity analysis
- Impact on 'bottom line'

APPENDICES

*Support analysis

7
FINANCIAL PROJECTIONS
- Revenue projections
- Expenditure projections
- Cash flow projections
- Projected balance sheets
- Profit projections

FIGURE 9.1

STEP 5—WRITING YOUR PLAN

9

> *The meaning of a message isn't totally controlled by its sender. The receiver's interpretation is equally valid.*
>
> Peter M. Lewis, *Guardian* 7th July 1993

All the hard work you have put into producing the first-cut of your plan will be squandered unless you can convert it into a finalized written form that is sufficiently appealing to your key readers to lead to their approval.

Figure 9.1 provides a template to help you write your business plan. In no way should you follow this template slavishly—it is critical that you adapt it and personalize it to reflect your own approach and the nature of the business you manage.

The main contents of this business plan are:

◆ Title page

◆ Summary

◆ Contents

1 Introduction

2 Outline of current business

3 Past performance

4 Vision

APPENDICES

List here the appendices you will need to provide support to your plan

1	
2	
3	
4	
5	
6	
7	
8	
9	
10	
11	
12	

FIGURE 9.2

5 Future plans

6 Financial implications

7 Financial projections

◆ Appendices

WRITING SEQUENCE

There is a perverse 'back-to-front' logic for writing your plan. In other words, do not start at the beginning and write your way through to the end. Rather, start at the end and work your way back to the beginning!

Bearing in mind that you have already prepared the first-cut of your plan, and that all your raw material and data is readily to hand, the suggested sequence for writing the final version is as follows.

◆ Appendices

7 Financial projections

5 Future plans

6 Financial implications

4 Vision

2 Outline of current business

3 Past performance

1 Introduction

◆ Summary

◆ Contents

◆ Title

FINANCIAL PROJECTIONS

Suggested outline text to start the section which summarizes the financial projections:

The overall results of implementing this business plan by moving towards the vision stated in Section 4 and achieving the strategic priority objectives stated in Section 5 are as follows:

	This year	Year 1	Year 2	Year 3
Revenue[1]	£800 000	£840 000	£920 000	£980 000
Costs[2]	£600 000	£660 000	£700 000	£740 000
Profit[3]	£200 000	£180 000	£220 000	£240 000

1 See Appendix 10
2 See Appendix 11
3 See Appendix 13

The decreased profit in Year 1 is due to our planned investment (see Section 5) in an additional computer system to handle the projected increases in our direct mail business together with an additional employee to work on this system.

And so on.

(The example above and figures are hypothetical.)

FIGURE 9.3

APPENDICES

To begin with, therefore, you will need to 'weed through' all your raw material and prepare a concise set of appendices which contain all the data and support analyses necessary to illustrate the key points at each step in your plan. These may include the following.

◆ Historical summaries of outputs and revenues

◆ Historical summaries of inputs and costs

◆ Historical balance sheets

◆ Historical summaries of profits

◆ Historical summaries of employee numbers

◆ Organization charts

◆ Summary career resumés of senior managers

◆ Outline of position in market (list of products, market share, etc.)

◆ List of competitors and competitive products

◆ Historical trends (key ratios, etc.)

◆ Projected outputs and revenues

◆ Projected inputs and costs

◆ Projected profits

◆ Projected cash flows

◆ Projected trends (key ratios, etc.)

◆ Sensitivity analyses

THE USE OF APPENDICES

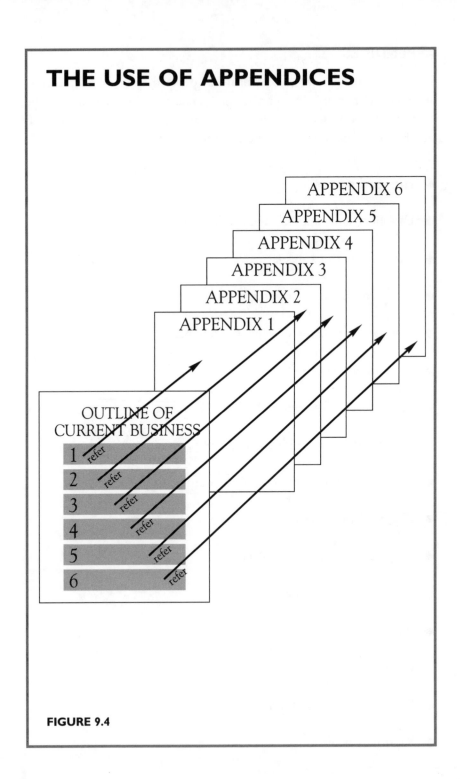

APPENDIX 6
APPENDIX 5
APPENDIX 4
APPENDIX 3
APPENDIX 2
APPENDIX 1

OUTLINE OF
CURRENT BUSINESS

1 refer
2 refer
3 refer
4 refer
5 refer
6 refer

FIGURE 9.4

The above data should not, in any way, clog up the main text which should flow effortlessly in a very readable and logical form. Only the 'bottom line' points should be referred to in the main text.

FINANCIAL PROJECTIONS

Having assembled the appendices, you are in a position to derive a summary of your overall projections and write the section which provides this. It is advisable to get to the point very quickly and summarize at the very outset the overall result of implementing your plan. You should then refer to your strategic priority objectives individually and demonstrate the financial impact each of these will have on your overall result. Figure 9.3 provides an illustration of this.

FUTURE PLANS

You can now write the section which details your strategic priority objectives, showing how you plan to convert your vision into achievable targets. You will need to make a case here for any major investments (in people, systems, equipment, etc.). At this stage there is no need to examine the financial implications of implementing your plans, therefore, aim to be very concise.

FINANCIAL IMPLICATIONS

Having justified your strategic priority objectives in the previous sections you should now devote a section to examining the financial implications of achieving each of these objectives.

The best way to do this is to analyse the financial consequences of pursuing each objective. Any assumptions you make should also be quantified. You will need to take into account the impact on revenue and costs of each of your planned decisions as well as to state clearly the assumptions you have made about pricing. It is also wise to provide a summary sensitivity analysis at this stage to demonstrate the risks involved should your assumptions fail to hold true.

WRITING THE SUMMARY

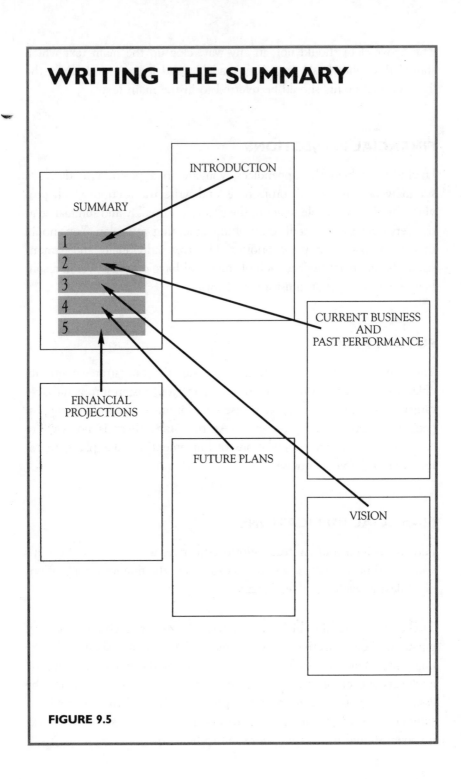

SUMMARY

INTRODUCTION

1
2
3
4
5

CURRENT BUSINESS
AND
PAST PERFORMANCE

FINANCIAL
PROJECTIONS

FUTURE PLANS

VISION

FIGURE 9.5

At the end of the section you should review and summarize these financial implications, stating the overall impact on the 'bottom line'. This will then flow neatly into the next section (Section 7) which you have just written.

VISION

It is important that your future plans (Section 5) and financial projections (Section 7) are underpinned by a clear vision for your business. Section 4 should be devoted to this.

There is no need to explain how you and the team arrived at the vision, though it is important to state that the vision has the support of your team. You will also need to state clearly the values and beliefs that you hold dear in the business. In other words this section summarizes, in very succinct terms, 'What we intend to be as a business'.

OUTLINE OF CURRENT BUSINESS

Much of the information about the current business can be confined to the appendices. It should suffice to provide an outline in this section, giving the reader who knows nothing about your business a broad but not detailed description of it. You will need to refer to your products and services as well as offering an overview of your customers, your competitors and your resources, together with the strengths and weaknesses you perceive in the business. It is also worth outlining your current management approach here.

Most importantly, it is worth providing a half-page summary (embodied in the main text) quantifying the key financial parameters of your current business. You can refer to the appendices for more detailed analyses of the current situation.

WRITING THE PLAN—SOME TIPS

◆ Create a clear structure
  (*so reader can find way around your plan*)
◆ Make it interesting
◆ Be totally objective
◆ Present it well
◆ Highlight key points
◆ Avoid jargon
◆ Minimize the use of acronyms
◆ Assume no 'inside' knowledge
  (*make everthing self-explanatory*)
◆ Take care when using your humour
◆ Never be personal
◆ Put all the boring stuff at the back
  (*use the appendices for data*)
◆ Don't make it too long
  (*20 minutes at first reading*)
◆ Don't patronize the reader
◆ Proofread at least three times—ideally with three different proofreaders
  (*eliminate sillly typing errors, grammatical slips, etc.*)

FIGURE 9.6

PAST PERFORMANCE

Some managers writing a business plan like to integrate this section with the previous section. Whichever approach you adopt, it is important that you devote a page or two to a record of your past performance—highlighting achievements over recent years as well as providing an analysis of historic levels of outputs, inputs, revenues, costs and profits.

This section, essentially, is your track record and is vital to establishing credibility and confidence in your ability to implement your recommended plan.

INTRODUCTION

This is the last main section you need to write. It should lay out the reasons for preparing the plan and the context within which it is written. It should also indicate what you are seeking to achieve in writing the plan. The introduction, in practice, sets the scene for the rest of the plan.

SUMMARY

You must provide a one-page (400 word) summary of the whole plan. This enables the busy reader to obtain an immediate 'feel' of what the plan is all about. The summary is the 'hook' which draws the reader into your document, which provides the key focus. Basically you should devote one paragraph (with a maximum of 80 words each) to each of the following sections in your summary:

◆ Introduction (reason for plan)

◆ Current business and past performance (credibility)

◆ Vision (what we intend to be)

◆ Future plans (things we plan to do)

◆ Financial projections (bottom line impact)

STYLE

Summarize here the personal style you
aim to adopt for your business plan:

_____

_____

_____

_____

_____

_____

_____

_____

FIGURE 9.7

STYLE

However you put the plan together it is critical that you impress your own personal style on it. This means presenting, in a unique way, your personal view of the business—past, present and future.

Too many plans are boring conglomerations of clogging statistics and bland intentions. You should aim to make your plan not only colourful but sharp—pointing the reader towards a convincing end result. Your plan must be readable and interesting with a clear, logical flow supported by well-made cases and invincible data and information.

Your plan should 'hum' with a combination of serious intent and excitement. Ideally, it should be spellbinding!

Some tips for writing the plan are provided in Fig. 9.6 on page 146.

PRESENTATION OPTIONS (THE GOOD, THE BAD AND THE UGLY!)

FIGURE 10.1

THE SUCCESSFUL MANAGER'S GUIDE TO BUSINESS PLANNING

STEP 6—PRESENTING YOUR PLAN

> ❝Any new strategy, no matter how brilliant or responsive will stand a good chance of not being implemented fully—or sometimes at all— without someone with power pushing it. . . . Empowering champions is one way leaders solidify commitment to a new strategy.❞
>
> Rosabeth Moss Kanter, *The Change Masters* 1984

Having written your plan, you now need to give some serious thought to the best way of presenting it. Your business plan is effectively a tool to help you 'sell the future' as you see it. As with any sales effort, presentation is of the essence.

There are two main factors to consider in presenting your business plan:

◆ The document itself and how it is put together.

◆ What you subsequently do with the document and the approval seeking process (selling the future).

THE DOCUMENT ITSELF

It is all too easy to turn off your reader with a document that is simply stapled together at the corner and soon falls apart, or is closely printed on poor quality paper and appears as a monotonous stream of endless paragraphs.

It is, therefore, worth devoting that little extra effort to produce a plan which not only makes for good and easy reading but is laid out in a professional way and is attractively bound with an eye-catching title page.

NEVER CRAM TOO MUCH ONTO ONE PAGE

The Successful Manager's Guide to Business Planning

The layout of each page of the plan should be equally attractive, using plenty of white space and a clear easy-to-follow structure. Never cram too much onto one page.

Use headlines for each section and subheadings to help your reader to find his or her way around your plan. Try to put as much of the detailed data into the appendices as possible so that you do not clog up the main text with too many tables and analyses. Where possible use simple 'boxed' tabulations and diagrams to present your summary data (referring to the details in the appendices).

A desktop publishing system will prove invaluable in helping you achieve the best layout and formats for your plan. If necessary take advice. Laying out a page is an art form and not everyone has the skill — it just might be that there is someone around who can do it better than you. Even be prepared to invest a little money in having a professional prepare the document for you. It is easy to ruin your future prospects by failing to spend a few pounds on presentation.

To help you decide on the best format take a look at some of the other documents, reports and plans you have on your shelves and in your filing cabinet. Look out for those that particularly appeal to you and try to establish

80

The Successful Manager's Guide to Business Planning

The layout of each page of the plan should be equally attractive, using plenty of white space and a clear easy-to-follow structure. Never cram too much onto one page.

Use headlines for each section and subheadings to help your reader find his or her way around your plan. Try to put as much of the detailed data into the appendices so that you do not clog up the main text with too many tables and analyses. Where possible use simple 'boxed' tabulations and diagrams to present your summary data (referring to the details in the appendices).

A desktop publishing system will prove invaluable in helping you achieve the best layout and formats for your plan. If necessary take advice. Laying out a page is an art form and not everyone has the skill — it just might be that there is someone around who can do it better than you. Even be prepared to invest a little money in having a professional prepare the document for you. It is easy to ruin your future prospects by failing to spend a few pounds on presentation.

To help you decide on the best format take a look at some of the other documents, reports and plans you have on your shelves and in your filing cabinet. Look out for those that particularly appeal to you and try to establish what makes them so special in your eyes. There is no copyright on layout and format — so don't be ashamed of pinching another style of presentation and perhaps using it as a basis for your own approach.

It is normally advisable to have your business plan bound rather than simply stapled together. This will put a final touch of class to the finished product. There are a number of inexpensive and easy-to-use binding techniques which are available on the market.

While the way the document is presented is all-important there is a danger in 'going over the top' with too much gloss. Good presentation is not synonymous with extravagance and expensive production. Again you will have to be the judge of how best to convey your ideas to your readers.

Overall your aim is to present your ideas in a way which is easy to follow, easy to understand and easy on the eye.

80

FIGURE 10.2

The layout of each page of the plan should be equally attractive, using plenty of white space and a clear easy-to-follow structure. Never cram too much onto one page.

Use headlines for each section and subheadings to help your reader find his or her way around your plan. Try to put as much of the detailed data into the appendices so that you do not clog up the main text with too many tables and analyses. Where possible, use simple boxed tabulations and diagrams to present your summary data (referring to the details in the appendices).

A desktop publishing system will prove invaluable in helping you achieve the best layout and formats for your plan. If necessary, take advice. Laying out a page is an art form and not everyone has the skill—it just might be that there is someone around who can do it better than you. Even be prepared to invest a little money in having a professional prepare the document for you. It is easy to ruin your future prospects by failing to spend a few pounds on presentation.

To help you decide on the best format, take a look at some of the other documents, reports and plans you have on your shelves and in your filing cabinet. Look out for those that particularly appeal to you and try to establish what makes them so special in your eyes. There is no copyright on layout and format—there is no shame in borrowing someone else's style of presentation and perhaps using it as a basis for your own approach.

It is advisable generally to have your business plan bound rather than simply stapled together. This will put a final touch of class to the finished product. There are a number of inexpensive and easy-to-use binding techniques available on the market.

While the way the document is presented is all-important, there is a danger in 'going over the top' with too much gloss. Good presentation is not synonymous with extravagance and expensive production. Again, you will have to be the judge of how best to convey your ideas to your readers.

SEEKING APPROVAL—CHECKLIST/PLAN

1 Complete final version of plan by:	
2 Produce distribution list	
3 Number of copies to be produced	
4 Decide on mode of presentation	
5 Prepare presentation by:	
6 Arrange presentation date	
7 Issue invitations to presentation meeting	
8 Rehearse presentation	
9 Distribute copies of plan	
10 Date of presentation	

FIGURE 10.3

Overall your aim is to present your ideas in a way which is easy to follow, easy to understand and easy on the eye.

APPROVAL SEEKING PROCESS (SELLING THE FUTURE)

Having produced the first bound copy of your business plan, you now need to decide how best to obtain the approvals you require. This is, essentially, selling your vision of your future to obtain support for it.

This is not as simple as producing (say) 12 copies of the plan, and distributing them to your boss and others in the organization you want to impress.

You need to prepare your approach carefully. There are a number of options to be considered:

◆ Convene a meeting of your key readers (those whose support or approval you need) and make a presentation to them (using overhead projection) having distributed copies of your plan to them a week or two **before**.

◆ Convene a meeting of your key readers (those whose support or approval you need) and make an overhead presentation to them, distributing copies of your plan to them **after** the presentation.

◆ Convene a meeting with your key reader (e.g. bank manager, director) and talk him or her through the plan, having sent a copy to him or her a week or two beforehand.

◆ Send a copy of the plan to your key readers, with a covering letter requesting a decision within a specified period of time.

Overall, you will stand the best chance of success with a personal presentation (with or without overhead projection) to your key readers. Your personal presence will add value to the substance of the plan, and enable your readers to raise questions with you and challenge the plan.

KEY POINTS

List here the key points you want to drive home during your presentation:

1	
2	
3	
4	
5	
6	
7	
8	
9	
10	

Remember:

in the presentation you will be 'selling'
your belief about the future of your business unit

YOU HAVE TO BELIEVE IT!

FIGURE 10.4

Ultimately, what you are selling is not your business plan but yourself. Effectively your plan is a reflection of your own thinking about your business—past, present and future. In other words, you are not seeking approval of a business planning document, but approval of your own thinking about the business, as clearly articulated in your plan. That articulation comes to life when you are able to talk it through with your audience.

Should you decide to give an overhead slide presentation it is important you take immense care to prepare a set of slides that captures your audience's attention—**not** mere copies of various pages in your plan. The slides should contain headline points only, together with summary tabulations and diagrams. Furthermore, any presentation you give should last no longer than 20 minutes. It is better to concentrate on the key points of your plan and leave your audience to raise questions of detail.

Treat such a presentation as a sales opportunity upon which your future livelihood depends—it does. Practice and practice, rehearsing it a couple of times in front of your team and your boss (if he or she is not the ultimate approver).

As stressed before, too many plans fall by the wayside because of poor presentation. It is dangerous to assume that pushing a poorly produced plan into the mail will achieve the desired goal of approval. Unless you take care, your plan may well just fall at the bottom of the heap and be forgotten. Or it might look so formidable (too many pages, too much data, too many words, poor layout) that the reader instinctively avoids getting down to read it!

Presenting your plan is a key step in the business planning process and will demand of you the highest degree of professionalism and skill.

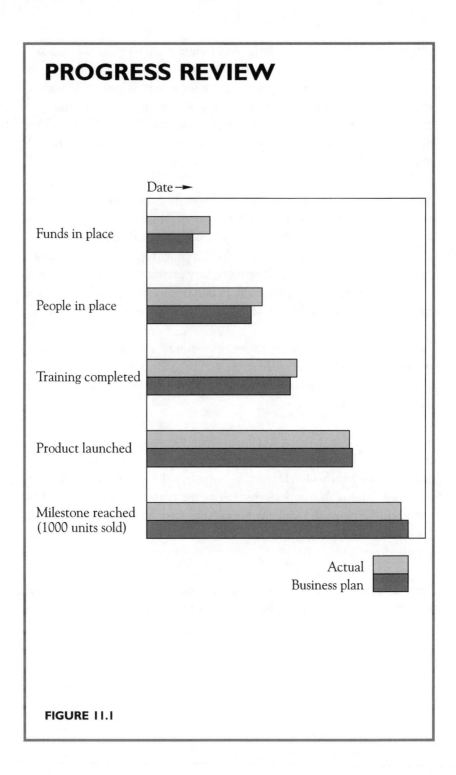

PROGRESS REVIEW

Date ➤

Funds in place

People in place

Training completed

Product launched

Milestone reached
(1000 units sold)

Actual
Business plan

FIGURE 11.1

STEP 7— IMPLEMENTATION AND REVIEW (FOLLOW-THROUGH)

11

> ❛We for a certainty are not the first
> Have sat in taverns while the tempest hurled
> Their hopeful plans to emptiness, and cursed
> Whatever brute and blackguard made the world❜
>
> A.E. Housman, *Last Poems* 1859–1936

Producing your business plan and getting it approved is easy in relation to achieving what is set out in the plan. In fact, the plan is worthless unless you use it as an 'implementation and review' tool.

You would not have produced a business plan and obtained approval of it unless you genuinely intended to achieve what it projects.

You will not achieve this unless you now use the plan as a basis for implementation and review. You will need to establish a clear process for doing this. There are three main priorities:

◆ Getting the people thing right

◆ Getting the money thing right

◆ Reviewing progress to make sure you got it right in the first place!

weekly summary

week [ ]

	OUTPUTS		REVENUE	
	ACTUAL	PLAN	ACTUAL	PLAN
Product 1				
Product 2				
Product 3				
Product 4				
Product 5				
Product 6				
Product 7				
Product 8				
Product 9				
Product 10				
TOTAL				

monthly summary

month [ ]

	OUTPUTS			REVENUE		
	ACT.	PLAN	YTD	ACT.	PLAN	YTD
Product 1						
Product 2						
Product 3						
Product 4						
Product 5						
Product 6						
Product 7						
Product 8						
Product 9						
Product 10						
TOTAL						

monthly cost summary

month [ ]

	INPUTS		COSTS	
	ACTUAL	PLAN	ACTUAL	PLAN
Input 1				
Input 2				
Input 3				
Input 4				
Input 5				
Input 6				
Input 7				
Input 8				
Input 9				
Input 10				
TOTAL				

cash flow summary

month [ ]

	CASH IN (revenue)	CASH OUT (expenses)	BALANCE
Brought forward			
Transaction 1			
Transaction 2			
Transaction 3			
Transaction 4			
Transaction 5			
Transaction 6			
Transaction 7			
Transaction 8			
Transaction 9			
Transaction 10			

annual projections

month [ ]

	OUTPUTS	REVENUE	COSTS	PROFIT
Product 1				
Product 2				
Product 3				
Product 4				
Product 5				
Product 6				
Product 7				
Product 8				
Product 9				
Product 10				
TOTAL				

FIGURE 11.2

PRIORITY I—GETTING THE PEOPLE THING RIGHT

You can only succeed in implementing your plan if you have the right people in place, and they are sufficiently skilled and motivated to work with you to achieve your strategic priority objectives and vision. By getting the 'people thing' right, everything else should follow.

A thousand books have been written on this vital topic—and still many senior executives get it wrong! You cannot afford to be one of them!

This is not the place to regurgitate all the basic principles and practices of effective people management. Having said that, it is essential that in embarking on the implementation of your plan you give careful thought to ensuring:

◆ that you have the right people in the right place to help you implement the plan.

◆ that every single person in your business unit is totally aware of the main components of the plan and is totally involved in implementing those aspects of it which have a direct impact on his or her job (to this extent you should carefully listen to any suggestions your people make about implementing the plan and take action accordingly).

◆ that everyone benefits from a carefully thought through programme of training and development, linked to the implementation of the plan.

◆ that you seize every possible opportunity to talk 'plan' with the people in your business unit.

	this week	last week	plan
OUTPUT 1	?	?	70
OUTPUT 2	?	?	75
OUTPUT 3	?	?	80
OUTPUT 4	?	?	75
OUTPUT 5	?	?	60
OUTPUT 6	?	?	65

It is inexcusable
not to meet your plan
for lack of adequate control information!

FIGURE 11.3

PRIORITY 2—GETTING THE MONEY THING RIGHT

If you fail to get the people thing right, your business will suffer a slow death. If you fail to get the money thing right, you will suffer a sudden death!

Whether you like it or not, money is the all-controlling factor in implementing your plan. Without gorging yourself on masses of useless statistics and data (as many managers do), it is essential, if you have not already done so, to establish some simple measures for monitoring and controlling the key financial parameters relating to the success of your plan.

These should include:

◆ A weekly one-page summary of actual outputs and revenue generated compared with plan.

◆ A more detailed monthly analysis of outputs and revenue generated compared with plan. This analysis should show results for the month as well as year-to-date.

◆ A detailed monthly analysis of inputs and costs compared with plan (again figures for the month as well as year-to-date).

◆ Weekly and monthly cash flows.

◆ Monthly projections (for the balance of the year) of outputs, revenues, costs and profit.

The above list is not exhaustive and of course should be adapted to your specific needs. If you are a manager of an internal business unit in a large organization (especially a public sector one) you may well struggle to receive weekly and monthly output data. The solution is simple—if the centralized system cannot provide you with the tools for the job, then you must create the tools yourself. **It is inexcusable not to meet your plan for lack of adequate control information**. When you are running your

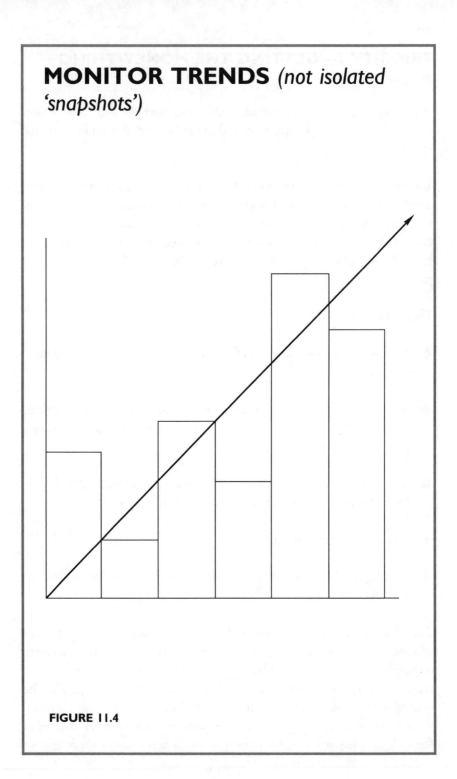

MONITOR TRENDS *(not isolated 'snapshots')*

FIGURE 11.4

own business it is essential to receive regular financial information for control purposes. You must imagine you are running your own business— and take action accordingly.

Having established a regular supply of useful financial information and analyses, it is important that you monitor the figures carefully. Again it is inexcusable if you fail to spot a serious fluctuation or a major deviation from plan. It is also inexcusable if you spot such a deviation and fail to take action. This does not mean a witch-hunt if you spot a shortfall, nor does it mean panic measures as if there were a crisis. What it does mean is some careful reflection with your team and your advisers about the appropriate action to get you back on plan.

You should aim to hold weekly half-hour meetings with your team to review the previous week's performance. A slightly longer meeting will be required after the end of the month. It goes without saying that the people who provide you with financial services should be committed to getting you the data and analyses within a day of the end of the week, or within a week of the end of the month. **Late data is as palatable as stale bread.**

In monitoring the 'money thing', look at trends and ratios rather than taking isolated snapshots. Never jump to conclusions or react precipitously—a careful finger on the pulse is called for—a sudden change in pulse rate does not necessarily indicate a heart attack!

PRIORITY 3—REVIEWING PROGRESS TO MAKE SURE YOU GOT IT RIGHT IN THE FIRST PLACE!

It is a truism to state that 'every plan is out of date as soon as it is written'. You can guarantee one thing about the future and that is your predictions of it will rarely be met. Circumstances inevitably change, unforeseen situations arise, luck intervenes—whether it be good or bad.

The unpredictability of the future does not invalidate the need for planning—it reinforces it. Planning is all about establishing a goal (your personal vision) and determining the best method of accomplishing it.

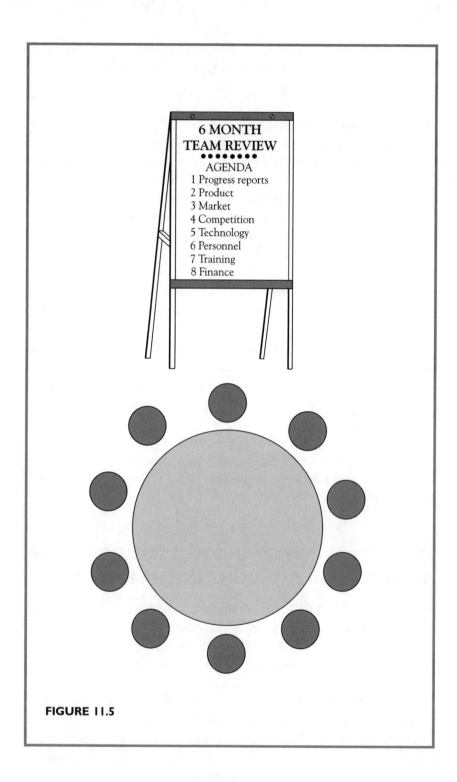

FIGURE 11.5

When unforeseen circumstances arise your goals do not have to change, though your methods of accomplishing them might. Inevitably there will be some occasions when you may even need to revise your goals. Even so, you will still need goals and methods of achieving them.

You will, therefore, need to review and revise your business plan from time to time, especially if you are using it as a basis for control.

It is worth getting together with your team every six months for a review of progress in implementing your plan, to establish deviations from plan and to chart corrective measures where necessary.

You will need to explore whether the original assumptions underlying your plan were correct, and whether you need to revise them and alter your strategic priority objectives accordingly. You will also need to take account of extraneous events—such as new competition and products coming onto the scene, advances in technology, changes in personnel, fluctuations in the economy, and political initiatives.

By the end of the first year, you will need to undertake a more thorough review and—in all probability—produce a revised version of your plan.

In other words, your plan is a living document requiring annual updating and amendments. As such, it will help you apply renewed direction, vigour and focus to your business.

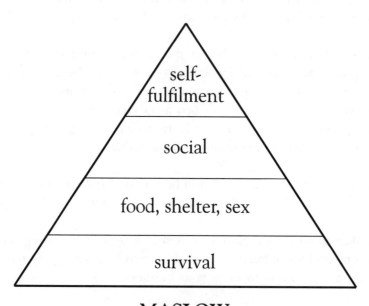

**MASLOW
HIERARCHY OF NEEDS**

FIGURE 12.1

BUSINESS PLANNING AND PERFORMANCE PAY

❝*If our original plan had had a lower goal we would have achieved less.*❞

William E. Foster, *Inc.* Magazine February 1987

❝*To accomplish great things we must not only act, but also dream, not only plan, but also believe.*❞

Anatole France

Those organizations that insist on having performance pay systems should consider using business plans as the vehicle for measuring accomplishments.

Over the last few years there has been much controversy about the issue of performance pay. It is fashionable to have performance pay schemes and, surprising as it seems, these have even been introduced in the public sector.

Regrettably, too many organizations fail to recognize the inadequacy of the schemes they have introduced. Their schemes manifestly do not achieve what they seek to achieve—an improvement in performance.

Students of personnel will readily quote the theories of Maslow and Herzberg to tell you that it is too simplistic to use the potential of increased pay as a prime motivator.

Too often performance pay schemes are perceived to be unfair and divorced from the actuality of real performance—using either artificial, simplistic and easy-to-gauge indicators or woolly subjective measures.

169

THE MYTH OF PERFORMANCE PAY

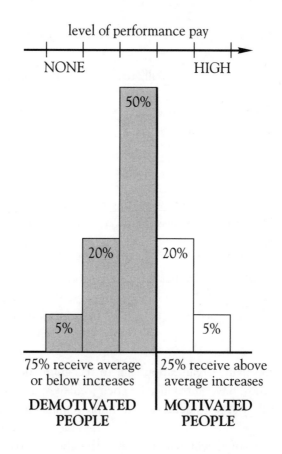

FIGURE 12.2

Too often these schemes lapse into a bureaucracy generated by retrenched personnel experts who realize their repressed creative potential with the introduction of another set of complex pseudo-scientific appraisal forms and glossy manuals to assist with completion.

The overall result is divisiveness and dissatisfaction, with only a minority of employees receiving the 'above average' merit pay expected by the majority. How demotivating to be told you are 'average' and can therefore only be rewarded with an average merit pay increase! Regrettably the majority of people are either average or below average.

Another consequence of performance pay is to encourage people to negotiate a suppression of their individual targets in order to maximize their chances of exceeding them to gain exceptionally high performance payments. Performance thus becomes an illusion more accurately reflecting negotiating skills than real accomplishment.

Performance pay can also prove a barrier to teamwork, with its frequent accent on **individual** achievement. The pursuit of such achievement by the individual is often done in a macho style and at the expense of colleagues in the team. Why waste time helping out your mates if your own performance bonus will suffer?

There is too much evidence and experience now to show that performance pay leads to argument and bad feeling for it to be denied. But, the solution is to hand!

If the term 'business' has any meaning it relates to the development of prosperity through commercial trade. The core idea of the 'business' concept is money. People trade to make money. People invest in businesses to make money. Money becomes a barometer of success—a reflection of achievement.

In other words, within the context of real business money is a motivator, whereas in a non-business context it cannot be. Most performance pay schemes fail because they are not integrated into the overall context of the business.

A SIMPLE BUSINESS LOGIC

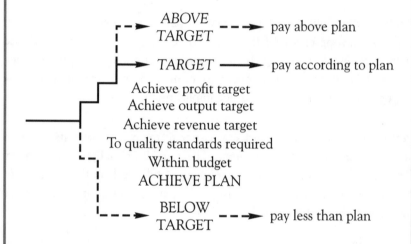

ABOVE TARGET ---> pay above plan

TARGET ---> pay according to plan

Achieve profit target
Achieve output target
Achieve revenue target
To quality standards required
Within budget
ACHIEVE PLAN

BELOW TARGET ---> pay less than plan

FIGURE 12.3

A business plan is therefore an excellent vehicle for pursuing a process of performance management. The successful implementation of the plan can be the basis for assessing real performance—and paying accordingly. If a self-employed business person does not trade there is no pay. Conversely, the more successful the trade, the greater the pay. The same principle should apply to the manager of a business unit and his or her team.

The measure of performance thus becomes very simple. It is the accomplishment of the strategic priority objectives in the business plan. It is important to stress that this is a business plan developed by the manager of the business unit. By definition, he or she should be highly committed to it, and so should his or her team. The advantage of using the business plan as a vehicle for performance pay is that there is no question of imposition.

The imposition and passive acceptance of substantial changes to the plan by senior executives will render it invalid. A business plan must be 'owned' by its originators. That ownership is denied when senior people force the originators to change the plan. That does not mean to say that in originating the plan the authors should not take into account the realities of normal organizational constraints. Inevitably the business plan of any local unit must be geared to the overall strategic aims of the organization as a whole. A business manager who ignores this when producing his or her plan is being blatantly unrealistic. But plans often go wrong when senior executives force business managers to shoot for unrealistic targets and force them to amend their plans accordingly.

Performance pay only becomes fair and reasonable when geared to a business plan totally owned by its originator and team.

Inevitably there will be an element of luck in the degree of success in implementing the plan. A business manager will have to accept a reduction in performance pay if luck turns against him or her. Such is life. A self-employed plumber whose van breaks down on the motorway cannot invoice for the work he planned, but failed, to do!

Business planning and management is all about attempting to control your own business destiny. Regrettably there will be times when your destiny seems to be out of control. Do not complain if your pay suffers as a result—the best business people survive the inevitable setbacks in life, recover quickly and go on to achieve great successes.

So the final (unnumbered) step in your business planning process is to work into your input costs a performance pay increase (for you and your team), geared to increased output revenue and profitability. To this extent the world is your oyster!

It would seem logical to most people that if you and your team were tremendously successful in implementing your business plan you should all reap an appropriate performance pay reward. Isn't that what business is all about?